James Noble   Ralph Johnson
Paris Avgeriou   Neil B. Harrison
Uwe Zdun (Eds.)

Transactions on Pattern Languages of Programming II

Special Issue on Applying Patterns

 Springer

Editors-in-Chief

James Noble, Victoria University of Wellington, New Zealand
E-mail: kjx@ecs.vuw.ac.nz

Ralph Johnson, University of Illinois, Urbana, IL, USA
E-mail: rjohnson@illinois.edu

Managing Editor

Uwe Zdun, University of Vienna, Austria
E-mail: uwe.zdun@univie.ac.at

Eugene Wallingford, University of Northern Iowa, Cedar Falls, IA, USA
E-mail: wallingf@cs.uni.edu

Guest Editors

Paris Avgeriou, University of Groningen, The Netherlands
E-mail: paris@cs.rug.nl

Neil B. Harrison, Utah Valley University, Orem, UT, USA
E-mail: neil.harrison@uvu.edu

Uwe Zdun, University of Vienna, Austria
E-mail: uwe.zdun@univie.ac.at

ISSN 0302-9743 (LNCS)   e-ISSN 1611-3349 (LNCS)
ISSN 1869-6015 (TPLOP)
ISBN 978-3-642-19431-3   e-ISBN 978-3-642-19432-0
DOI 10.1007/978-3-642-19432-0
Springer Heidelberg Dordrecht London New York

Library of Congress Control Number: 2011921520

CR Subject Classification (1998): D.2, D.3, D.1, K.6, K.6.3

Typesetting: Camera-ready by author, data conversion by Scientific Publishing Services, Chennai, India

Printed on acid-free paper

Springer is part of Springer Science+Business Media (www.springer.com)

Preface

Even though patterns are a software engineering success story and have become mainstream in recent years, the application of the different types of patterns in practice has not yet fully met the expectations of the patterns community. Among other reasons, this is due to the inefficient advertisement of patterns to the practitioners' community, as well as the lack of techniques and tools for using patterns, and for introducing them into organizations. There are many pattern enthusiasts in the industry but the large body of patterns knowledge is not fully exploited in practice. Many practitioners are aware of the GoF patterns and use them regularly in design and coding, but there is substantially less evidence of the systematic use of patterns in other areas of software, such as software architecture, analysis, or processes. While there are many anecdotes of the benefits of using patterns, the impact of using patterns is not fully understood yet. We note that there is some increase in teaching patterns in higher education and professional training programs, but the results are only slowly becoming visible in industry.

We are interested in studying the application of patterns in practice both from the practitioners' and the researchers' point of view. Practitioners such as experienced architects and designers have applied pattern-based approaches in industrial projects and have shown promising results even if they lack scientific rigor. Researchers have proposed scientific approaches that aim at methods in software engineering or other domains in order to support the systematic application of patterns but may still be at the research stage.

We initiated an effort to gather together practitioners and researchers working on this topic by organizing a special track on the European Conference on Pattern Languages of Programs in the years 2008, 2009, and 2010. The track received ample interest from the patterns community and received a number of high-quality submissions, containing a mix of practical and research approaches. It provided encouraging results and a strong indication that the application of patterns is an important topic for the community at large. The other positive development is that some of the papers discussed in this track have included empirical validation in an attempt to provide evidence about the effectiveness of the proposed approaches. In this special issue we have included five papers which are characteristic of this theme in applying patterns both from researchers and practitioners.

In less than two decades since software patterns were introduced, their effect on software development has been remarkable, particularly with respect to object-oriented design patterns. Object-oriented design patterns have become mainstream: they are widely used, college courses on patterns are common, and design pattern expertise even appears as a desired skill in job position descriptions.

Outside the realm of the OO design patterns, the picture is somewhat cloudier: patterns other than OO design patterns are not as well known. This is partly due to the profound success of the design patterns book. Nonetheless, there are numerous other categories of patterns, and some of them enjoy widespread use in individual organizations or domains (e.g., distributed computing and enterprise applications).

But how much use do patterns have? And how beneficial are they? Unfortunately, the evidence of the utility of patterns is still largely anecdotal. This is even true of the vaunted design patterns: everyone agrees that they are the greatest thing since curly braces, but we aren't sure exactly how much they improve design. This is not exclusively a problem within software patterns; the quality of software designs is notoriously difficult to measure. Furthermore software designers' intuition is indeed worth something: if many designers swear by patterns, they are probably right. However if we aim at convincing organizations about the benefits of applying patterns, we have to follow rigorous approaches and provide hard evidence rather than relying on anecdotes and gut feeling. This is in line with the software engineering community's attempt to turn towards evidence-based software engineering in order to have a more profound impact on the state of practice.

Therefore, there is a need to examine the use of patterns in industrial settings, collect data, and provide evidence to answer questions on how to use patterns as well as their benefits and liabilities. Thus one purpose of this special issue is to explore the usage of patterns in the real world. A related purpose is to continue to spread knowledge of particular patterns so that best practices also become ubiquitous practices.

The articles in this issue all demonstrate techniques for applying patterns in an industrial or research setting. Some have confronted the topic within software engineering; others offer approaches in other pattern domains, which is an indication of the diverse fields where patterns are applied.

In "Lessons Learned from Using Design Patterns in Industry Projects," Dirk Riehle elaborates on his long-term experience in applying design patterns in industrial projects and subsequently affecting the organizational culture. Riehle explains the main benefits that design patterns bring in software development: communication, implementation, and documentation. He then suggests the introduction of a design language that is specific to an organization, which codifies the collective reusable knowledge about patterns extended from design to implementation. Finally he presents specific lessons learnedand guidance for creating and applying such a design language using study groups and writers' workshops. The evidence collected from the author's experience demonstrates benefits for the organizations involved and justifies the investment required.

In "Choose Your Own Architecture – Interactive Pattern Storytelling", Jim Siddle proposes the concept of interactive pattern stories as a way to use patterns in the education of software engineers and especially designers. The idea behind interactive pattern stories is to enrich traditional pattern stories with some interactivity by having the readers make decisions and follow different paths through the story. The author presents an example interactive pattern story, which uses patterns from the distributed systems domain. The approach enables readers to explore various alternative solutions to design problems and reflect on the solutions' benefits and liabilities. The interactive format used in this approach is engaging and game-like, though it requires substantial effort to write the stories' format. The applicability of the approach is mostly within higher software engineering education or professional training.

In "Experiences in Using Patterns to Support Process Experts in Process Description and Wizard Creation", Birgit Zimmermann, Christoph Rensing, and Ralf Steinmetz propose the use of patterns as a means to codify expert knowledge in adaptation processes and semi-automate the knowledge transfer. Their approach starts with the creation of process patterns for a specific application domain: adapting e-learning material. The knowledge stored in the process patterns through a specific formalism is then used to semi-automatically generate wizards that can eventually guide the end users step-by-step to perform the adaptations. The approach has been empirically validated in an industrial setting with promising results. This is one of the few approaches that consumes the knowledge (about processes) within patterns and semi-automatically creates tooling to support processes.

In "Modifiers: Increasing Richness and Nuance of Design Pattern Languages", Gwendolyn Kolfschoten, Robert O. Briggs, and Stephan Lukosch tackle one of the major challenges in using patterns: the tradeoff between a rich pattern language that provides a plethora of inter-dependent solutions and the cognitive over-load that large pattern languages may cause. Especially novices learning a pattern language may get overwhelmed by the number of choices and the rich dependencies between them. The authors propose to resolve this with the concept of the modifier: a variation that can be applied to a set of other patterns. Modifiers result in similar modifications to the solutions of all the patterns within the set of patterns to which they are applied. The concept of a modifier is exemplified with two case studies: two different pattern languages for facilitation and computer-mediated interaction. The approach has been validated through expert judgment that yielded positive results.

In "Patterns for Effectively Documenting Frameworks", Ademar Aguiar and Gabriel David present best practices for documenting object-oriented frameworks in pattern form. They present six documentation patterns as well as many details on how to apply these patterns in practice. In particular, a pattern-based documentation process covering the major roles and activities of object-oriented framework documentation is presented. In addition to this process, guidelines are given concerning why, by whom, to whom, and when framework documentation should be performed and a detailed pattern sequence is given clearly outlining the relationships of the patterns. Finally, various issues of framework documentation and the types of information to be documented are systematically discussed.

Patterns have always been about capturing best practices in software so that others may benefit from them. Yet for this very reason, the practical use of any pattern predates its discovery. This must be so, because patterns are proven solutions – they have already been used multiple times before they can be considered patterns. In this sense, people use patterns in two ways: intentionally, based on their knowledge of the patterns, and unknowingly. The ongoing challenge, therefore, is to bring the hitherto unknown patterns to light. And it is a challenge: there are so many patterns that have already been written, along with others to be written, that finding the patterns that are most important for a designer at a particular moment is daunting. We hope that searching the vast landscape of patterns will become more viable through organization of patterns, searching tools, and the continued emergence of domain-specific patterns. We have no illusions that this will be easy. And it is made more difficult by the continued emergence of new patterns, as more and better ways of developing software are devised. But the prospect of these new patterns is indeed a happy thought.

We advocate patterns as a cost-effective way to transfer knowledge, establish communities of practice that share this knowledge, and solve problems based on sound reasoning instead of intuition and trial-and-error attempts. However, the second and even greater challenge to pattern adoption is to accompany the patterns and pattern languages with the appropriate evidence about their effectiveness and the support they can provide to practitioners. Introducing patterns into an organization or into a project is an investment; therefore it has to be justified with the appropriate evidence. Consequently we make a plea to practitioners and researchers alike, to gather such evidence and disseminate it across the community. There are numerous stories about using patterns in the field; it is our responsibility to share them and reinforce our collective knowledge.

December 2010

Paris Avgeriou
Neil B. Harrison
Uwe Zdun

Table of Contents

Lessons Learned from Using Design Patterns in Industry Projects

Dirk Riehle

SAP Research, SAP Labs, LLC
3412 Hillview Ave, Palo Alto, CA 94304, U.S.A.
dirk@riehle.org
www.riehle.org

Abstract. Design patterns help in the creative act of designing, implementing, and documenting software systems. They have become an important part of the vocabulary of experienced software developers. This article reports about the author's experiences and lessons learned with using and applying design patterns in industry projects. The article not only discusses how using patterns benefits the design of software systems, but also how firms can benefit further from developing a firm-specific design language and how firms can motivate and educate developers to learn and develop this shared language.

Keywords: Design pattern, pattern language, design language, design communication, design collaboration, design implementation, design documentation.

1 Introduction

The notion of design pattern has been defined as the abstraction from a common solution to a recurring design problem in a given context [1] [2]. A well-known example is the Observer pattern from the Design Patterns book (a.k.a. the "gang of four" book [1]) which solves the problem of managing state dependencies between objects through the introduction of registration and callback interfaces.

A design pattern like Observer introduces terms like "observer" and "subject" that become part of the language that developers speak when they go about designing, implementing and documenting software systems. This article discusses different uses of design patterns and how to be effective at them. The article is based on the author's experiences with using and applying design patterns in industry projects since 1995 (Section 2). The discussion focuses not only on design patterns, but also on the overall vocabulary and language that a software development team or a firm typically speaks. The article shows how design patterns can fit into such a design language, the firm's software architectures, and its programming practices.

Prior work has shown how a firm can benefit from using and applying design patterns [7] [11] [12]. This article discusses how these benefits can be enhanced further through the development and use of a firm-specific design language (Section 3 and 4). Such a firm's design language is something that needs to be learned and that keeps evolving. New employees need to be brought up to speed with the language and new insights need to work their way into the language. Hence, this article presents the author's experiences with running study groups and other educational measures that

J. Noble et al. (Eds.): TPLOP II, LNCS 6510, pp. 1–15, 2011.

are used to make new employees become more productive faster. Finally, the article presents experiences with advanced study groups and writers' workshops to refine a firm's understanding of its own software patterns and architecture (Section 5).

2   Base of Experiences

The experiences presented in this article are based on the author's involvement with the industry projects shown in Table 1. The author was employed full-time with the respective firm pursuing the project.

Table 1. List of projects the author was involved in from 1995 to 2006

Firm	Project Name	Time Frame	# Developers	Author's Role
UBS	KMU Desktop	1995-1996	13	Developer
UBS	KMU Desktop	1996-1998	15	In-house Consultant
KMU Desktop stands for "Kleine und Mittlere Unternehmen" i.e. small and medium-size businesses. This is a banking application for commercial lending [32] [31].				
UBS	GBO Project	1997-1999	7	In-house Consultant
GBO Project stands "Global Business Objects" and was an attempt to consolidate the globally distributed applications of UBS, a Swiss Bank, under one object model [32] [34].				
Skyva	Skyva	1999-2002	15	Architect
Skyva	Skyva	1999-2002	45	In-house Consultant
Skyva was the name of both the company and its software product for managing supply chains. The author's team focused on the core language, runtime, and tools for a UML virtual machine [33]. The author consulted to all of development, 45 developers in total.				
Bayave	Bayave	2004-2006	5	Chief Architect
Bayave Software GmbH develops on-demand business software for small businesses.				

The core of the experiences reported about is based on the time frame from 1995-2002 when the author started systematically introducing design patterns into the software development processes he was involved in.

After leaving UBS and joining Skyva, the author made specific choices and consulted in-house to foster the creation of a firm-specific design language based on design patterns. His later work at Bayave repeated some of those experiences.

Typically, the author was both a developer and/or architect and an in-house consultant, to build trust and to ensure his feet were on the ground.

Since 2006, the author has only been involved with smaller research projects that did not influence the experiences presented in this article in any significant way.

3   Uses of Design Patterns

This section reviews the key uses of design patterns the author has found in industrial software development projects. It also discusses some common misconceptions.

The dominant uses of patterns in software development are to facilitate

- communication,
- implementation (by hand),
- and documentation of software systems

as documented before [7] [10] [11] [12] [13].

In addition, some research and development efforts have gone into pattern-based code generation, which is now supported by commercially available tools like IBM Rational's Software Modeler or Borland's Together. However, the pattern-oriented features of these tools have yet to reach maturity, in particular in their expressiveness for capturing design patterns as well as in their support for round-trip engineering. In the author's opinion, design pattern based code generation has not had any significant impact on the industry's design practices; the article discusses some of the reasons for this in Section 3.4 on misconceptions.

3.1   Communication

By far the dominant use of design patterns the author has seen in his projects is in informal and creative communication between software developers [13] [7]. Working on a white-board or discussing a design at the water cooler, developers use pattern-based vocabulary to refer to their prior and shared design experiences as well as the generally known descriptions of one or more patterns. By referring to such prior experiences, developers bundle knowledge about design constraints, the contexts in which they apply, and their solution in one apt name. They use this knowledge in evaluating and deciding on design options to solve the design problems at hand.

Consider Figure 1. Here, on a white-board, a developer might be explaining to a colleague how he intends to handle incoming user requests to a web server in such a way that these requests can be undone, bundled into multi-step requests, made persistent, and replayed at some later time on some other server. The developer explains how he encapsulates a request as a command object, how he creates composite command objects to bundle atomic steps into more comprehensive actions, and how a command processor keeps track of the sequence of overall user actions such that multi-step undo and replay becomes possible.

The second developer, who knows the Command, Composite, and Command Processor patterns [1] [3] and who has previously used these patterns, is likely to grasp the idea of the design quickly. She proceeds to provide feedback, points to problems and suggests alternative solutions, using equally refined professional language. In the well-known back and forth of a creative discussion, design patterns make software developers more efficient and more effective. This is simply because they need fewer words to refer to comprehensive problem solutions and yet remain clear about what they are saying while using design ideas that have been proved to work well.

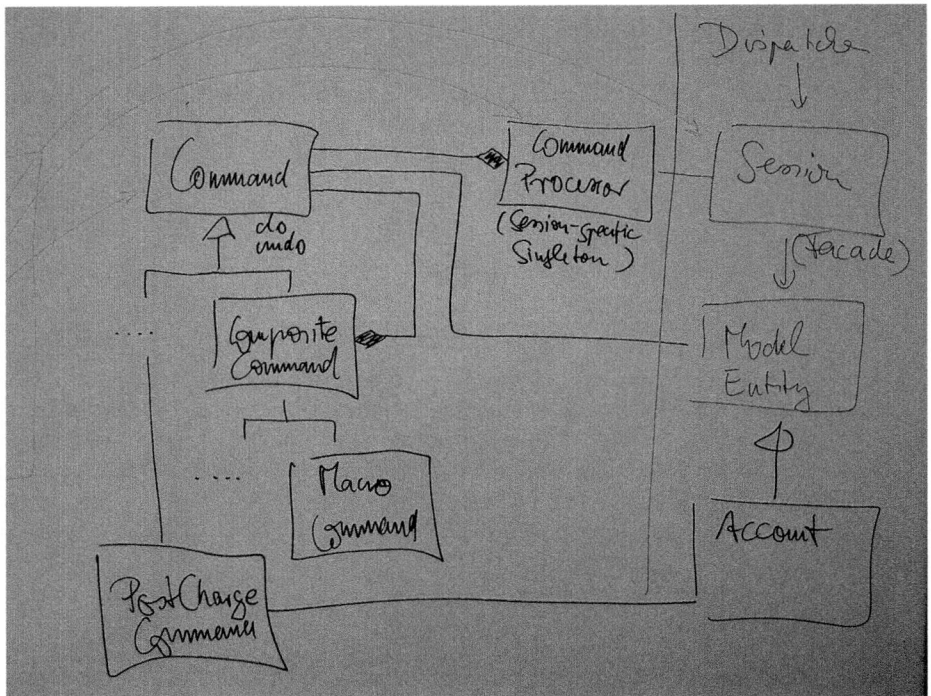

Fig. 1. An illustration of a design described using the Command and related patterns

The goal of using design patterns in informal communication is to make developers more effective. In the author's projects, developers typically settled quickly into a work mode where ambiguities are removed as they surface by refining what has been said. Completeness and correctness were not primary goals. The point was to have a discussion that lead to an incomplete but shared understanding of some design aspects of the overall system. This shared understanding allowed developers to continue on their paths, working forward, and reconvening as they run into problems with the design some time down the road.

3.2   Implementation

The second most important use of design patterns lies in implementing software systems. One misconception with design patterns is that they are on the "design level" only and are disconnected from the code. This is clearly not true [4] [7] [22] [25]. Design patterns, as the descriptions in the Design Patterns book vividly show, are closely connected to code [1]. There is not a single design pattern description in the seminal work that doesn't come with comprehensive code examples. This is not to say that there is only one way of turning a pattern into source code (see Section 3.4 on common misconceptions). An experienced developer has multiple templates in the back of his or her mind that he uses and adapts as he translates the results of a design discussion into code.

Consider the white-board discussion from Section 3.1. After the developers decide that the sketched-out design is a good way forward, the first developer returns to his workstation to define the interfaces and class structures, followed by an initial implementation and some test cases. While writing the code, the developer balances in his head the specifics of the discussed design, the canonical implementations described in the respective pattern descriptions, some other implementations that only this developer may have seen, and the general needs of the problem at hand. During this implementation, the developer faces design and implementation problems that were not discussed with the other developer, but that come up as he is working on the code. Most of these problems are solved on the spot using informed judgment, but a few may be so tricky that they are left unsolved and reserved for future discussion with other developers.

The role of design patterns in this activity is to inform the details of writing source code: What methods to group together and to put on what interface or class, what the exact signature of a method should look like, in what order to call other methods, and so on. Design patterns inform such decisions, because they provide a more comprehensive "bigger" picture of the design and yet are specific enough to lead to code based on prior experiences. In the example from Section 3.1, the developer has to decide whether the undo/redo methods of the Command interface are visible to everyone or only the CommandProcessor, whether the addChildCommand method is on the Command or CompositeCommand interface, and so on.

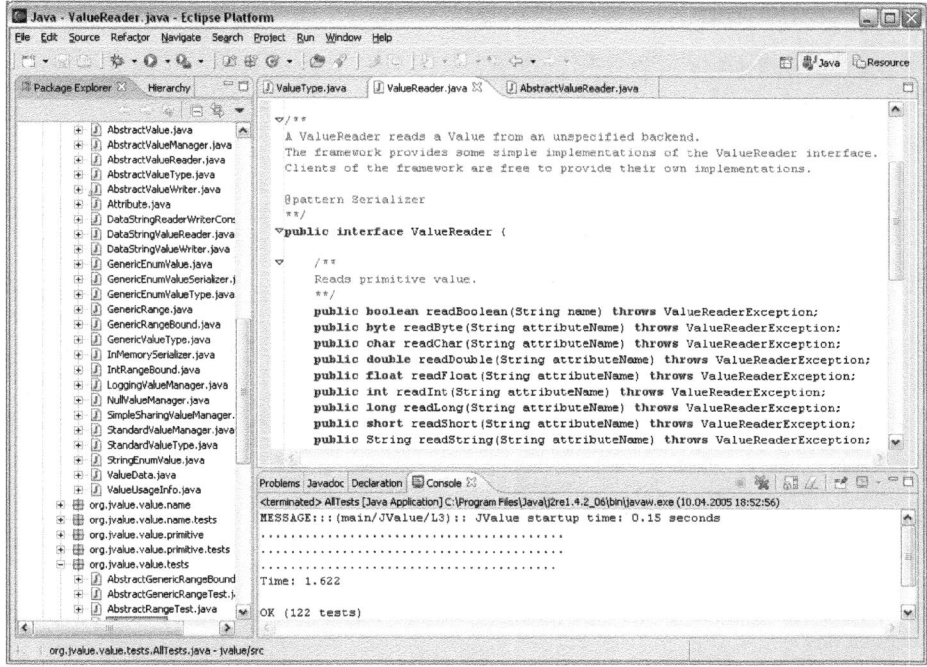

Fig. 2. The ValueReader interface of the Serializer pattern implementationin the JValue framework

Figure 2 shows the ValueReader interface from the Serializer design pattern implementation in the JValue framework for Value Objects [14] [15] [16]. A developer familiar with the Serializer pattern can immediately recognize the purpose of the interface and derive the structure and behavior of its implementations.

In the author's projects, experienced software developers used their knowledge of design patterns and their implementation variants on a continued on-going basis to transfer a design into code. This benefits everyone: Because other developers know these stylized design pattern implementations as well, they can more quickly understand from the code which pattern is being implemented and what the consequences for the system's structure and behavior are. Thus, using and applying design patterns made implementing designs and comprehending source code easier.

3.3 Documentation

The third main use of design patterns the author has found is to aid documentation. For example, in a typical word processor document, a developer might describe a design by showing its class structure. He or she explains that the class structure implements a set of design patterns and then shows how that structure achieves its purpose by referring to the elements of the design patterns, their structural relationships, and their protocols of interaction. Basically, design patterns give a developer a vocabulary that he can use to document a design in a more succinct way than possible with only regular prose.

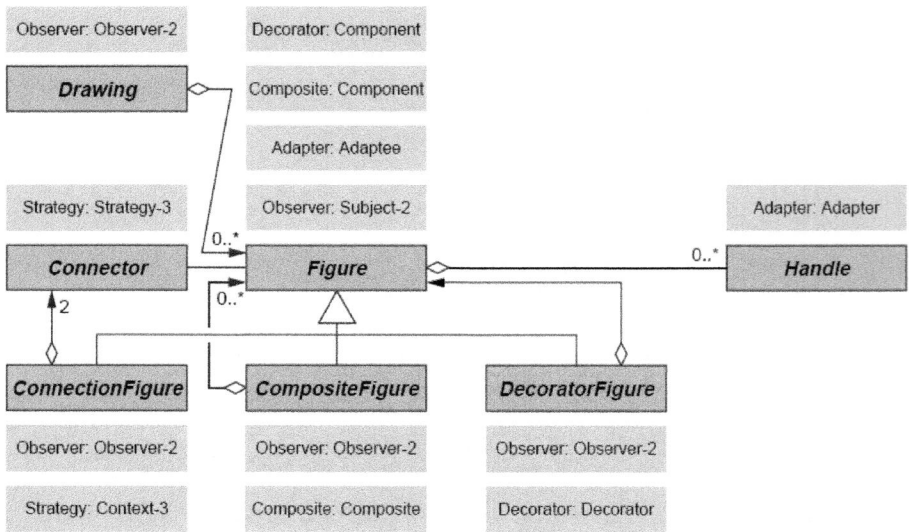

Fig. 3. Documentation of the core design of the JHotDraw frameworkusing design pattern annotations

Figure 3 illustrates such informal documentation using a design pattern annotation form suggested by Erich Gamma [10]. The figure displays several core classes from the JHotDraw framework for graphical editors [17]. A blue box next to a class annotates the class as playing a particular participant role in the pattern application, as described in the original design pattern documentation. Where it says "Observer: Subject-2" the Figure class plays the Subject role from the Observer pattern. It says '2' because there is more than one application of the Observer pattern in this design (not shown in Figure 3).

In some projects, developers documented object-oriented designs in a more formal fashion using UML tools. UML's design pattern feature was used to annotate collaborations as design pattern instances. Frequently, the author found that developers took these class diagrams from the UML tool and copied them over into a word processor document or a wiki where they were explained in prose again. Wherever or whatever the master document, the lesson is clear: Experienced developers use design patterns to express the structure and dynamics of their designs. It speaks to them and those who are reading the design.

Like in design pattern guided implementation, it is the author's experience that using design patterns in documenting designs makes developers more effective and helps readers comprehend designs faster.

3.4 Misconceptions

By far the most common mistake that surfaced in the projects was to confuse a design pattern with a design template or even a code template. This mistake is easy to make; after all, the structure diagram in the Design Patterns book suggests that there is only one particular structure that is to be considered as the pattern. This is an incorrect interpretation. The structure diagram in the Design Patterns book is an illustration of the most common form the pattern may take when it gets applied, but it really is only one of many forms [1] [4] [10], as confirmed by John Vlissides, one of the authors of the Design Patterns book [22].

Figure 4 shows three different structure illustrations of the Composite pattern. The first one is the structure diagram of the original description. The second one is discussed as a variant in the implementation section of the original description. The third one is a variant of the pattern used in one of the firms the author worked for. (See Section 4 on firm-specific design languages.) All three illustrations are truthful to the idea and description of the Composite design pattern.

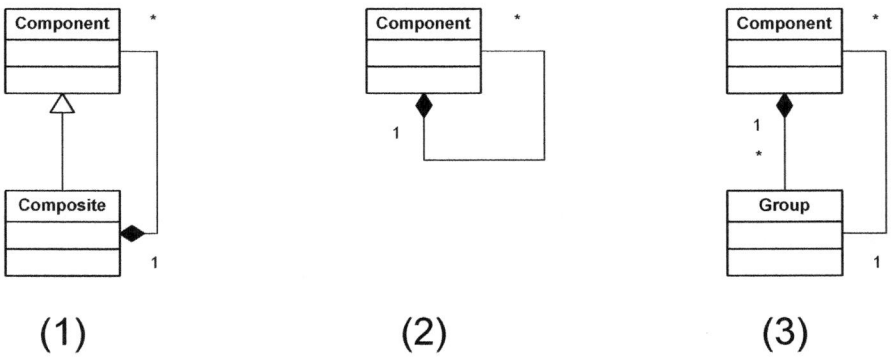

Fig. 4. Three different illustrations of common variations of the Composite design pattern

It is important to note that these illustrations are just that: illustrations. There is no well-defined pattern specification language underlying these class diagrams. These diagrams are specific designs with classes that have general names for the purpose of invoking the idea of how an application of the pattern could look like: They are an illustration, not a (formal and precise) specification.

It should not come as a surprise that design patterns can be implemented in different ways. Not even the authors of the Design Patterns book could foresee all the possible circumstances in which to find a solution to a recurring problem. For example, the Design Patterns book was written when multi-threading was less common than today; thus, most of the patterns ignore this contextual force. In a multi-threaded context, however, the Singleton pattern is likely to fail when implemented as illustrated in the book. For the successful use of the Singleton pattern in multi-threaded applications, according to this author's experience, the notion of single exemplar needs to be changed to a context-specific singleton, which typically leads to a rather different implementation.

The UML 2.0 specification suggests using the modeling concept of Collaboration to illustrate design patterns. However, UML collaborations are limited in many ways. First, the notion of a pattern in UML is that of a specific (template-like) design element and is therefore too specific to allow for the many variations in which a pattern can come. Second, the notion of pattern in UML is constrained to collaborations, that is, descriptions of how objects collaborate to achieve some purpose. The author's work on using collaborations (a.k.a. role models) to describe patterns [5] supports the idea that many design patterns are best viewed as abstractions from recurring collaborations between objects. However, not all patterns are behavioral in nature. The Null Object pattern, for example, is wholly structural [18] and cannot be illustrated well by the UML notion of pattern.

To resolve the conflict between the original notion of a pattern as an idea that may take many forms and the desire to have exactly one precise specification, the author's projects have found it useful to distinguish between a design pattern, its variations, templates for those variations, and implementations or applications of those templates [6] [13]. A pattern is the idea that solves a problem, and that idea can show itself in many different variations, depending on the context. Formal specifications of these variations are viewed as templates that can be instantiated to give users a specific design and a specific implementation. The relationship between pattern and template is 1-to-n, and the relationship between template and application is 1-to-n as well. This distinction solves the conflict between the desire to formalize and the need for flexibility.

4 A Firm's Design Language

The author's projects benefited from using and applying design patterns as discussed in the previous section. However, the projects went further: They adapted design patterns and design vocabulary to their specific processes and products. The author saw this happening in the projects at UBS and he actively supported and steered this process while working at Skyva and Bayave, see Table 1 and Section 5. This section discusses the additional benefits projects harvested from investing into project and firm-specific design languages.

Design patterns are an important part of the language that experienced software developers use when talking about system design and implementation. Other components of this language that the author found are

- project and firm-specific variations of design patterns,
- project and firm-specific patterns discovered in the firm's products and systems,
- the architecture of the firm's products and systems, and
- the firm's programming practices.

In a well-working software organization, these parts come together to form what the author of this article, inspired by [8] [23], is calling a "design language". A design language consists of the words and concepts that developers use to effectively communicate about the design and implementation of their work products. It is rooted in everyday natural language and enhanced by the technical concepts developers are dealing with in software design.

4.1 Firm-Specific Pattern Variations

Recall the definition of design pattern given in the introduction: "An abstraction from a common solution to a recurring design problem in a given context." Often neglected, understanding a pattern's context is important. This is because the forces that represent a context shape what a good solution for the problem is.

In a firm that provides a particular product or system that system and its requirements represent the main set of forces, or context, of any pattern application. The system and its architecture, whether it is object-oriented, event-driven, or data-flow-oriented, details many of the forces and leads to firm-specific variations of design patterns. These are general design patterns that have found a specific recurring variation in the system or product of a software organization.

Figure 4 shows variations of the Composite pattern. The Composite pattern lets developers represent and manage an object tree. Each object is a component (node in the tree), and some components are composite objects consisting of further component objects, some of which may be composites, etc. An object tree emerges from this common problem solution.

On the right, Figure 4 shows a firm-specific variation of the Composite pattern that was used at Skyva. Rather than having components (nodes) maintain links to their sub-components (child nodes), an intermediate Group object maintains these links. Thus, a component has a group object which in turn holds the links to the next lower level of objects in the tree.

This indirection may seem like unnecessary complexity in the general situation, however, it was a necessity for the meta-data driven software system under development. This system had a description layer that determined the system structure at runtime and could also change at runtime. For that reason, it couldn't be known exactly how many different types of trees an object might be a node in. Rather, the developers had to assume it could be any number. An example of such a situation is the modeling of a firm's organizational structure. Here, one may need to represent a person's position in many different hierarchies: First, there is the regular line reporting hierarchy, then there maybe any number of projects each of which introduces its own reporting hierarchy, there may be a technical reporting relationship, etc. Organizational modeling is one situation where this design pattern variant is used, business process modeling is another.

The firm-specific variation shown in Figure 4 solves this problem by letting a node have multiple group objects, each of which provides access to the sub-nodes in a different tree. You can see this by the 1-to-n relationship between Component and Group in the UML diagram of this pattern variation.

For the project at Skyva, recognizing this variation of the Composite pattern as a firm-specific variation of the pattern represented a major step forward. We quickly standardized our vocabulary on terms like Component and Group and became more effective at discussing our designs wherever this pattern variation showed up.

4.2 Firm-Specific Design Patterns

It is not just variations of known patterns: At Skyva and Bayave the developers also found new and not yet documented patterns. Developers documented them when they felt they were relevant for their work. At Skyva, the author's team not only discovered the Composite pattern variation of Figure 4, but also discovered what was called the Navigator pattern. The Navigator pattern describes a generalized traversal algorithm over an object graph using meta-data to find the next target of the navigation. The team used "a navigator" to find a particular component in the graph. Using "navigator" and ancillary terms, the team could quickly and effectively discuss its designs.

Later the author's team learned that this pattern could also be found in implementations of the XPath/XQuery specification, which are a part of most XML processing engines these days. Hence, what was thought of as a firm-specific pattern apparently was not, and there were other people who had discovered the same pattern or at least were using it.

It is likely that a firm-specific pattern or a firm-specific pattern variation isn't that firm-specific after all and can be generalized. However, as long as there is no generally known description of these patterns available, a firm does well to come up with its own description (see Section 5.2 on study groups). Once more, the lesson that the author learned was that recognizing patterns and standardizing vocabulary makes developers more effective.

4.3 Firm-Specific Architecture and Coding Practices

A firm's design vocabulary and language comprises not only design patterns but also architecture and programming. It is not important whether an architectural style is called an architecture pattern or whether a coding trick is called a programming pattern [7]. What is important is that a firm's developers recognize a recurring theme as such and develop a common vocabulary around it, most likely by writing up the pattern and discussing it among themselves.

Prior work has shown how firms can benefit from using design patterns [11] [12]. During his work at UBS, the author observed that using design pattern terminology is part of a more comprehensive domain- and firm-specific language that developers speak when going about their work. At Skyva then, as well as at Bayave later, he explicitly developed this language using an on-going elicitation process. Uncommon terms, or common terms with specific meanings, were called out and discussed and documented on the firm's wiki, just like the design patterns.

In the author's experience, developing and maintaining a shared firm-specific design language can enhance the benefits derived from using design patterns greatly. When asked how design patterns had helped them, developers almost always provided positive responses. When asked how important the firm-specific design language was, responses were always enthusiastic, because the design language was custom-made to support the projects' daily work routines and usually did so well.

5 Learning the Language

During the work at UBS it had became clear that projects could become more effective by developing and using a shared design language. However, it was unclear what exactly the language consisted of and how to learn and refine it. Consequently, at Skyva, the author experimented with different forms of learning and reflection [8] to help new developers learn the design language, to refine the language together with experienced developers, to promote design patterns, and to discover yet hidden patterns.

The main vehicles of helping learning and reflection employed are

- individual tutoring,
- study groups (a.k.a. reading groups) [19] and
- writers' workshops [9].

Both the study groups and the writers' workshops groups were both internal and external to the firm, serving different purposes.

5.1 Individual Tutoring

In the author's experience, an open and collaborative atmosphere that encourages sharing of design ideas, discussion of these ideas, and conclusions that lead to standardized vocabulary requires an atmosphere of trust, where ideas are welcome and everyone benefits.

The best way that to create this atmosphere is to lead by example and to give ideas and experience away freely. Whenever a new developer got on board, the author would sit down with the developer, helping them understand design patterns in general as well as our firm-specific variations.

This demonstrated the value of design patterns and that the firm cares about it. Once a new developer recognized these benefits, the developer was ready to join the foundational study group. The study group in turn would relieve the author and other senior technical members of the team from the time burden that such tutoring creates.

5.2 Study Groups

A study group is a voluntary typically weekly get-together of 1-2 hours that would study a pattern or paper. At Skyva, the author instituted two types of study groups. One studied well-established foundational material like the Design Patterns book, and one covered new and advanced patterns, concepts, and techniques.

The first type of study group, the foundational study group, tried to get new people up to speed, both on general as well as firm-specific material, including but not restricted to design patterns. Through this study group and the ensuing discussions, developers automatically soaked up the firm's language, as the natural thing was to discuss and discover applications of the design patterns in our day-to-day work.

The author has found that the following aspects were critical to making a study group a success and to maintain its momentum:

- At least one senior technical member of the team participated and facilitated the study group;
- The material chosen for review was relevant to the participants' work;
- Senior management clearly supported the study group and its activities.

This type of study group started over after about a year. There was no fixed curriculum, but the material the group reviewed was generally foundational and included patterns from the Design Patterns book. Members could join and leave as they pleased, and the group had many developers attending only sessions of particular interest to them.

The second type of study group, the advanced study group, reviewed current material from outside the company like new patterns from the annual Pattern Languages of Programming conference. In addition, the advanced group reviewed and discussed new material from the firm itself in a writer's workshop, see Section 5.3.

Firm-internal study groups can learn from outside efforts. The longest running cross-firm patterns study group that the author is aware of is the Silicon Valley Patterns group [20]. When asked by the author of this article, the group provided the following best practices for keeping the study group alive and interesting [21]:

1. Bring in authors (of the material under review)
2. Provide a safe setting (in particular, stop trouble makers early)
3. Say your names (to create a community atmosphere)
4. Insist on preparation (so meetings can be effective)
5. Encourage everyone (so nobody feels left behind)
6. Reflect and experiment (with the way the group works)
7. Meet in a comfortable place (in a cafe, not at work!)
8. One person at a time (give everyone room to speak)
9. Bring in laptops (to gather material or experiment on the side)
10. Select by consensus (so the group supports the curriculum)

The author of this article can confirm the Silicon Valley Patterns group experiences from his own study groups. Additional lessons learned in the author's firm-internal study groups were:

- Have a motivated group leadership that sticks with the group
- Be current on what's going on and bring it into the group
- Have a good connection to authors and don't be afraid to invite them
- Have at least one good moderator and facilitator
- Welcome everyone and discourage arrogance
- Organize through a mailing list and/or a wiki
- Meet consistently and regularly

The firm-internal study groups that the author started had no end date but just kept meeting regularly. There was always something new to discuss. Of particular interest were patterns that came out of the firm itself, enhancing and sharpening the firm's design language.

5.3 Writers' Workshops

Study groups typically study other people's material. Writers' workshops are a means for studying someone else's work with the goal of providing the writer with candid feedback [9]. In a writers' workshop, writer joins a group of readers who are reviewing the writer's work. The writer is not allowed to speak but can observe how workshop participants struggle with the material. From this, the writer learns how to improve the material. Richard P. Gabriel brought writers' workshops into the patterns community, where they have become an important part of patterns conferences [24].

In all cases, this article's author introduced writers' workshops to his firm-internal advanced study group meetings with the goal of developing and refining firm-specific material. The aforementioned Composite pattern variation and the Navigator pattern, as well as other published patterns like Value Object, Serializer, and Role Object went through such writers' workshops and benefited greatly, both in terms of contents and presentation.

A firm-internal workshop can be pragmatic, and pattern descriptions and other materials can be run through it multiple times, before they are considered polished documentation. Feedback always included both form and contents. The author has found participants to be quite enthusiastic about it, mostly because they were familiar with the material and the examples and can provide excellent feedback, refinement, and generalization.

The firm itself benefits from better documentation, a standardized vocabulary, and in the end more effective software developers.

6 Related Work

The main body of this article already mentions most of the related work, and this Section summarizes it and relates it to the work presented in this article.

In general, the usefulness of patterns in software systems design has been anecdotally reported about many times [1] [3] [6] [7] [10] [11] [12].

Also, many have reported on the breadth of applicability of patterns [2] [3] [7] [13] [24] that goes beyond design and extends to architecture and programming as well as specific domains like user interfaces and business processes [24] [27] [28] [29] [30].

Other disciplines have made a case for design languages and a broader focus on the vocabulary used in innovation and design [8] [10] [23] without necessarily applying this thinking to software design or design patterns.

This article goes beyond this related work by summarizing the benefits of using and applying software patterns, as learned in industry projects (Section 3). It extends these experiences into the broader realm of design languages, which have been considered and worked upon, but to the best of this author's knowledge not in this form for software design (Section 4). Finally, this article presents specific lessons learned and guidance for using and applying design patterns through building up firm-internal know-how around a firm's design language using study groups and writers' workshops (Section 5). While study groups and writers' workshop have been researched in general, to the best of this author's knowledge they have not been as coherently integrated with the software development process and the use and application of design patterns as presented in this article.

7 Conclusions

Core activities of software development like design discussions on a white-board, implementation of such designs in code, as well as their documentation can greatly benefit from design patterns and the shared vocabulary they provide. Effective use of design patterns depends on avoiding common mistakes like those that equate a design pattern with its structure diagram and generated code. Combined with other software design concepts and embedded in a firm's design language, patterns are an important contribution to making software development more effective. This article confirms prior work on the general benefits of using design patterns and adds to it experiences with developing and maintaining a firm-specific design language. Such a design language needs to be nurtured through study groups and writers' workshops. The experiences of this article's author show that such a design language can make software development even more effective and more enjoyable than possible with standard design patterns alone.

Acknowledgments

I would like to thank the anonymous reviewers for helping me improve this article.

References

1. Gamma, E., Helm, R., Johnson, R., Vlissides, J.: Design Patterns. Addison Wesley, Reading (1995)
2. Alexander, C., Ishikawa, S., Silverstein, M.: A Pattern Language. Oxford University Press, Oxford (1977)
3. Buschmann, F., Meunier, R., Rohnert, H., Sommerlad, P., Stahl, M.: Pattern-Oriented Software Architecture. Wiley, Chichester (1995)
4. Zdun, U., Avgeriou, P.: Modeling Architectural Patterns Using Architectural Primitives. In: Proceedings of OOPSLA 2005, ACM Press, New York (2005)
5. Riehle, D.: Composite Design Patterns. In: Proceedings of OOPSLA 1997. ACM Press, New York (1997)
6. Riehle, D.: The Perfection of Informality: Tools, Templates, and Patterns. Cutter IT Journal 16(9), 22–26
7. Riehle, D., Züllighoven, H.: Using Patterns in Software Development. TAPOS 2(1) (1996)
8. Schön, D.: The Reflective Practitioner (1983)
9. Gabriel, R.P.: Writers' Workshops and the Work of Making Things. Addison Wesley, Reading (2004)

10. Vlissides, J.: Pattern Hatching. Addison-Wesley, Reading (1998)
11. Beck, K., Coplien, J.O., Crocker, R., Dominick, L., Meszaros, G., Paulisch, F.: Industrial Experience with Design Patterns. In: Proceedings of the 18th International Conference on Software Engineering. IEEE Press, Los Alamitos (1996)
12. Schmidt, D.C.: Experience Using Design Patterns to Develop Reusable Object-Oriented Communication Software. Communications of the ACM (October 1995)
13. Buschmann, F., Henney, K., Schmidt, D.C.: Pattern-Oriented Software Architecture. On Patterns and Pattern Languages, vol. 5. John Wiley and Sons, Chichester (2007)
14. Riehle, D.: "Value Object". In: Proceedings of the 2006 Conference on Pattern Languages of Programming (PLoP 2006). ACM Press, New York (2006)
15. Riehle, D.: The JValue Framework for Java Value Objects, http://www.jvalue.org
16. Riehle, D., Siberski, W., Bäumer, D., Megert, D., Züllighoven, H.: Serializer. In: Pattern Languages of Program Design 3, ch. 17, Addison-Wesley, Reading (1998)
17. Gamma, E.: JHotDraw, http://www.jhotdraw.org
18. Woolf, B.: Null Object. In: Pattern Languages of Program Design 3, ch. 1, Addison-Wesley, Reading (1998)
19. Kerievsky, J.: A Learning Guide to Design Patterns, http://www.industriallogic.com/papers/learning.html
20. The Sillicon Valley Patterns Group, http://www.siliconvalleypatterns.org
21. Bialik, T., Ruffer, R.: Personal Communication (2005)
22. Vlissides, J.: Personal Communication (2001)
23. Brand, S.: How Buildings Learn: What Happens After they are Built. Penguin (1994)
24. Coplien, J., Schmidt, D. (eds.): Pattern Languages of Program Design. Addison-Wesley, Reading (1995)
25. Avgeriou, P., Zdun, U.: Architectural Patterns Revisited – A Pattern Language. In: Proceedings of the 10th European Pattern Languages of Programming Conference. Universitatsverlag Konstanz (2005)
26. Harrison, N.: Organizational Patterns for Teams. In: Pattern Languages of Program Design 2, Addison Wesley, Reading (1996)
27. Vlissides, J., Coplien, J., Kerth, N. (eds.): Pattern Languages of Program Design 2. Addison-Wesley, Reading (1996)
28. Martin, R., Riehle, D., Buschmann, F. (eds.): Pattern Languages of Program Design 3. Addison-Wesley, Reading (1998)
29. Harrison, N., Foote, B., Rohnert, H. (eds.): Pattern Languages of Program Design 4. Addison-Wesley, Reading (2000)
30. Manolescu, D., Voelter, M., Noble, J. (eds.): Pattern Languages of Program Design 5. Addison Wesley, Reading (2005)
31. Riehle, D., Schäffer, B., Schnyder, M.: Design of a Smalltalk Framework for the Tools and Materials Metaphor. Informatik/Informatique, 20–22 (February 1996)
32. Riehle, D.: Framework Design: A Role Modeling Approach. Dissertation, No. 13509. Zürich, Switzerland, ETH Zürich (2000)
33. Riehle, D., Fraleigh, S., Bucka-Lassen, D., Omorogbe, N.: The Architecture of a UML Virtual Machine. In: Proceedings of the 2001 Conference on Object-Oriented Programming Systems, Languages, and Applications (OOPSLA 2001), pp. 327–341. ACM Press, New York (2001)
34. Bischofberger, W., Guttman, M., Riehle, D.: Global Business Objects: Requirements and Solutions. In: Mätzel, K.-U., Frei, H.-P. (eds.) Proceedings of the 1996 Ubilab Conference, Zürich, pp. 79–98. Universitätsverlag Konstanz, Konstanz, Germany (1996)

"Choose Your Own Architecture" - Interactive Pattern Storytelling

James Siddle

Independent
jim@jamessiddle.net
http://www.jamessiddle.net

Abstract. The concept of Interactive Pattern Stories is introduced as a way to support software design education. An example interactive pattern story is presented, along with benefits, liabilities, and applicability of the approach. Key benefits include enabling readers to explore different choices to design problems and to experience positive and negative consequences of design choices, and the engaging game-like format. The key liability is the complexity of the writing task. The main application area is to education and learning.

Keywords: Patterns, software patterns, pattern stories, interactive fiction, software design, software architecture.

1 Introduction

> *"You peer into the gloom to see dark, slimy walls with pools of water on the stone floor in front of you. The air is cold and dank. You light your lantern and step warily into the blackness. Cobwebs brush your face and you hear the scurrying of tiny feet: rats most likely. You set off into the cave. After a few yards you arrive at a junction. Will you turn west (turn to 71) or east (turn to 278)?"* - Step 1 of "The Warlock of Firetop Mountain" [1].

This paper proposes the concept of *interactive pattern stories*, as a way of supporting the exploration of pattern-based designs in an engaging, educational, and fun way. The *"Choose Your Own Adventure"* [2] style of book is proposed as a suitable basis for introducing interactivity into *pattern stories*.

An example interactive pattern story, presented below, is used to show the benefits of this medium to software design education. The interactive story, based on a previously published story, is interactive around design alternatives, illustrates the consequences of different design choices, and allows exploration pattern-based designs.

The rest of this paper is structured as follows. The target audience is introduced, followed by an introduction to pattern and interactive fiction concepts. The origin and structure of the interactive story is then described along with the key benefits offered to software design education. Reader guidance provides essential information to interactive story readers, then the interactive story itself

J. Noble et al. (Eds.): TPLOP II, LNCS 6510, pp. 16–33, 2011.

appears. Next, an analysis of story features, benefits, liabilities, and applicability of the approach is presented. The paper closes with an overview of related and further work, and conclusions.

1.1 Target Audience

Computer science students, software developers, and software architects will gain insight into the application of patterns, choices available during software design, and will learn several desirable and undesirable design choices related to request handling. Patterns theorists and authors will learn how to combine interactive fiction and pattern concepts to create interactive pattern stories for patterns-based education. Technical writers may benefit from learning an interactive approach to describing the design and development of software through patterns.

2 Concepts

2.1 Patterns, Pattern Stories, Pattern Languages

A *pattern* [3] is a solution to a problem that occurs in a particular context, captured in an easy to understand format. A *pattern story* [4] describes the application of one or more patterns. Pattern stories can be derived from *pattern languages* [3], which connect patterns together to provide guidance in solving wider problems than is possible with individual patterns. A key feature of pattern languages is that patterns are connected together via a shared context, where the application of one pattern creates a context in which another pattern can be applied.

To apply a pattern language, one follows the connections in the language to build up a *sequence* [4] of patterns. Each pattern application solves one part of the overall problem, after which the reader determines the next sub-problem they want to tackle (the pattern texts help with this). The reader then follows a connection from one of the patterns they have already applied, to solve the next part of the overall problem. This continues until the reader's overall problem has been fully solved, or the pattern language is unable to help the reader further.

Note however that patterns and associated structures, concepts and approaches are not a silver bullet for designing software - for example a pattern or pattern language may only cover part of the problem space for a given context, leaving the designer with a partial solution. The quality of a design derived from a pattern language is dependent on how extensive and rich the language is. Additionally, effective use of patterns relies on the designer treating them as design guidance rather than prescriptive solutions; the designer must use his or her knowledge of the specific problem being faced to fill in the gaps in any particular pattern.

2.2 "Choose Your Own Adventure" and Interactive Fiction

"Choose Your Own Adventure" [2] books are a form of children's literature which is interactive in nature. The reader typically starts at a single entry point which describes the overall context for the story, then is presented with several decisions each of which lead to further story, and further decision points, etc.

Eventually the reader will come to one of many endings, some good, others bad. For an in-depth examination of interactive fiction see *"Twisty Little Passages: An Approach to Interactive Fiction"* by Nick Montfort [5].

3   Interactive Pattern Stories

3.1   Origin of the Story

This paper presents an interactive story based heavily on a "request handling" pattern story published in *"Pattern-Oriented Software Architecture, Volume 5: On Patterns and Pattern Languages"*[1] [6]. In this story, a collection of patterns are applied to create a framework for handling requests. Various problems are posed, such as how to encapsulate or uniformly handle requests, and various patterns are applied to solve the problems. This pattern story was originally derived from the pattern language published in [7].

Rather than write a completely new interactive story from scratch, the request handling story was transformed into the interactive version that appears below. The text was reworded into second-person (a defining characteristic of interactive fiction stories), and decisions and associated consequences were introduced into the tail end of the story.

3.2   Story Structure

The story is structured around decisions that the reader makes, relating to the STRATEGY, TEMPLATE METHOD, NULL OBJECT, and COMPOSITE COMMAND patterns.

The narrative, design choices, and consequences in different story paths are derived from variations to the request handling story suggested by the story authors (see [8]), as well as pattern descriptions and connections found in the pattern language in [7].

Additionally, the story is based around a fixed set of functional and quality requirements, which the reader is expected to fulfil. In the story, the functional requirements - a system's capabilities, services, and behaviour [9] - must always be fulfilled. The quality requirements - the qualities of the system being developed that are influenced by design decisions taken [9] - vary according to the reader's choices.

3.3   Key Benefits of the Approach

The benefits of the approach to readers are:

- The ability to explore different solutions to design problems.
- They can experience both positive and negative consequences of design choices.
- They will be engaged by the game-like format.

These benefits are explored in section 6.3 below.

---

[1] Frank Buschmann, Kevlin Henney, Douglas C. Schmidt. Copyright 2007, John Wiley & Sons Limited. Reproduced with permission.

4   Guidance for the Interactive Story Reader

4.1   Requirements

The interactive story is based around two functional requirements, and three quality requirements. The functional requirements will always be fulfilled, whilst the quality requirements may or may not be fulfilled based on your actions. The text of the story describes the consequences of your design decisions in relation to the quality requirements.

You may wish to refer back to this point when you are presented with choices in the story to refresh your memory.

Functional Requirements

- **Requirement F1:** Support for an optional logging policy mechanism to allow requests that are handled by the framework to be logged in a variety of ways. This mechanism is expected to be used to allow different qualities of service (such as the level of detail provided) for different deployments of the request handling framework.
- **Requirement F2:** The ability to create compound requests, to support composition of commands that have been written to be processed by the framework.

Quality Requirements

- **Requirement Q1:** Developers and users of the framework should find it easy to work with (*understandability*).
- **Requirement Q2:** It should be easy to perform routine maintenance of framework and framework-using code, such as fault correction or performance improvement (*maintainability*).
- **Requirement Q3:** It should also be easy to take advantage of new software or hardware technologies that may become available in the future (*evolvability*).

Note that functional requirement references are denoted below with an *F*, quality requirements with a *Q*.

4.2   How to Read the Story

Start reading at step 1, which provides the context for the story[2].

Make sure you are familiar with the requirements presented above, then simply follow the decision instructions as they appear. A route map for the story can be found in the appendices, along with thumbnails for each pattern used.

---

[2] In addition to those listed above, other functional requirements apply to step 1. These are not explicitly listed to ensure the information presented is relevant to the interactive portions of the story.

A few other things to bear in mind are:

- The decisions presented are intentionally short on information to keep each story succinct, and to promote exploration of the design options. Under ideal circumstances, design decisions would be based on an assessment of all relevant information, this is rarely the case on real projects so the decisions do represent realistic choices.
- A valid option at each decision point is to go back a step - most software projects employ some form of source control, allowing earlier versions of source code to be reverted to. Please take this as an implicit option that simplifies the presentation of available options.
- Similarly, the choices presented do not represent the entire set of decisions available, rather a subset chosen to enable exploration of software design in the particular context. In reality, software professionals are always free to make whatever choice they wish. More experienced or advanced practitioners may find the choice constraints limiting.

5   The Interactive Story

Step 1

You are developing an extensible request-handling framework for your system, and are faced with the problem of how requests can be issued and handled so that the request handling framework can manipulate the requests explicitly.

You decide to objectify requests as COMMAND objects, based on a common interface of methods for executing client requests. COMMAND types can be expressed within a class hierarchy, and clients of the system can issue specific requests by instantiating concrete COMMAND classes and calling the execution interface. This object can then perform the requested operations on the application and return the results, if any, to the client.

The language chosen for implementing the framework is statically typed, and there may be some implementation common to many (or even all) COMMANDs in your system. You wonder what the best form for the COMMAND class hierarchy is.

You decide to express the root of the hierarchy as an EXPLICIT INTERFACE. Both the framework and clients can treat it as a stable and published interface in it's own right, decoupled from implementation decisions that affect the rest of the hierarchy. You decide that concrete COMMAND classes will implement the root EXPLICIT INTERFACE, that common code can be expressed in abstract classes below the EXPLICIT INTERFACE rather than in the hierarchy root, and that concrete classes are expressed as leaves in the hierarchy.

You realise that there may be multiple clients of a system that can issue COMMANDs independently, and wonder how COMMAND handling can be handled generally.

You decide to implement a COMMAND PROCESSOR to provide a central management component to which clients pass their COMMAND objects for further handling and execution. The COMMAND PROCESSOR depends only on the EXPLICIT INTERFACE of the COMMAND hierarchy.

You also realise that the COMMAND PROCESSOR makes it easy to introduce a rollback facility, so that actions performed in response to requests can be undone. You extend the EXPLICIT INTERFACE of the COMMAND with the declaration of an undo method (which will affect the concreteness of any implementing classes), and decide that the COMMAND PROCESSOR will handle the management.

After introducing the undo mechanism, you recognise that there is also a need for a redo facility, to allow previously undone COMMAND objects to be re-executed. You need to determine how the COMMAND PROCESSOR can best accommodate both undo history and redo futures for COMMAND objects.

You decide to add COLLECTIONS FOR STATES to the COMMAND PROCESSOR, so that one collection holds COMMAND objects that have already been executed - and can therefore be undone - while another collection holds COMMAND objects that have already been undone - and can therefore be re-executed. You make both collections into sequences with 'last in, first out' stack-ordered access.

You understand that some actions may be undone (or redone) quite simply, but that others may involve significant state changes that complicate a rollback (or rollforward). You wonder how the need for a simple and uniform rollback mechanism can be balanced with the need to deal with actions that are neither simple nor consistent with other actions.

You decide to allow COMMAND objects to be optionally associated with ME-MENTOs that maintain whole or partial copies of the relevant application state, as it was before the COMMAND was executed. You also decide that those COMMAND types that require a MEMENTO will share common structure and behaviour for setting and working with the MEMENTO's state. You express this commonality by introducing an abstract class that in turn implements the COMMAND's EXPLICIT INTERFACE; MEMENTO based COMMAND types can then extend this abstract class. COMMAND types that are not MEMENTO based won't inherit from this abstract class, implementing the EXPLICIT INTERFACE directly, or extending another abstract class suitable for their purpose.

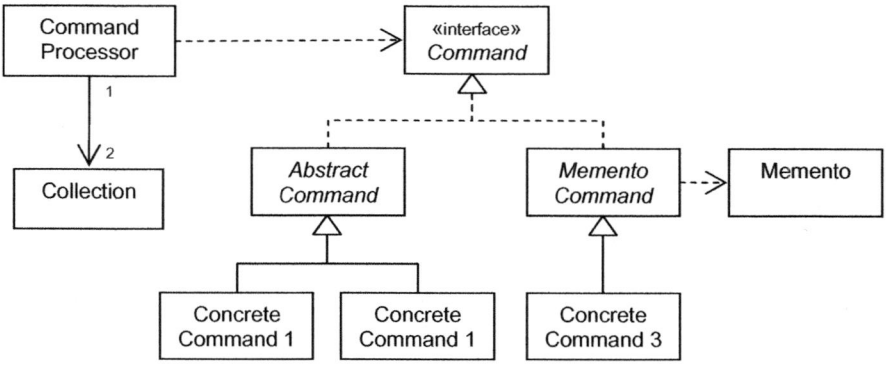

Fig. 1. UML diagram of the software described so far

The UML diagram in figure 1 shows the software decribed so far.
Now continue at step 2...

Step 2

You now realise that the framework needs a logging facility for requests, and wonder how logging functionality can be parameterized so that users of the framework can choose how they wish to handle logging, rather than the logging facility being hard-wired.

If you wish to use inheritance to support variations in housekeeping functionality, turn to 7.
Otherwise if you prefer the use of delegation, turn to 3.

Step 3

You choose to express logging functionality as a STRATEGY of the COMMAND PROCESSOR, so that a client of the framework can select how they want requests logged by providing a suitable implementation of the STRATEGY interface. This ensures that the common COMMAND PROCESSOR behavioural core is encapsulated in one class, while variations in logging policy are separated into other classes, each of which implements the STRATEGY interface.

Clients of the request handling framework can select how they want logging performed by choosing which STRATEGY to instantiate the COMMAND PROCESSOR with. Some users will want to just use the standard logging options, while others may wish to define their own custom logging, so you ensure the framework provides some predefined logging types.

This clean separation supports the understandability (Q1), maintainability (Q2), and evolvability (Q3) of both the framework and any additional logging policy classes introduced as part of concrete deployments.

Having introduced a parameterized logging facility, you wonder how the optionality of logging can be realised, in the knowledge that it makes little functional difference to the running of the framework.

If you wish to make changes to the COMMAND PROCESSOR control flow to take account of optionality, turn to 8.
Otherwise if you prefer a more transparent solution, turn to 4.

Step 4

You provide a NULL OBJECT implementation of the logging STRATEGY which doesn't do anything when it is invoked, but uses the same interface as the operational logging implementations. This selection through polymorphism ensures that you don't need to introduce difficult to understand control flow selection within the framework to accommodate the optional behaviour, and ensures understandable (Q1) and maintainable (Q2) framework code.

Turn to 5.

Step 5

Your request handling framework is almost complete; but you still need to ensure that compound requests are handled. Compound requests correspond to multiple requests performed in sequence and as one; they are similarly undone as one. The issue you face is how compound requests can be expressed without upsetting the simple and uniform treatment of COMMANDs within the existing infrastructure.

If you want to create a special kind of COMMAND *to deal with all compound requests, turn to 6.*

Otherwise, if you're happy for compound requests to be handled by the framework as it stands, turn to 9.

Step 6

You decide to implement a compound request as a COMPOSITE COMMAND object that aggregates other COMMAND objects. To initialise a COMPOSITE COMMAND object correctly, you ensure that other COMMAND objects (whether primitive or COMPOSITE themselves) must be added to it in sequence.

This special type of COMMAND enables arbitrary compound requests to be created and composed, simplifying use of the request handling framework and avoiding the need for complex, tightly coupled, dedicated compound request classes - enhancing the maintainability (Q2) and evolvability (Q3) of client code. This comes at the cost, however, of a reduction in the understandability (Q1) of framework code - COMPOSITE [10] implementations can be complex and non-obvious.

Turn to 10.

Step 7

You decide to introduce a logging TEMPLATE METHOD to the COMMAND PROCESSOR class, then call the abstract method whenever logging is required within the COMMAND PROCESSOR. By necessity, you make the COMMAND PROCESSOR class abstract.

Logging policies are provided through subclasses of the COMMAND PROCESSOR, ensuring that common behaviour is encapsulated in a superclass, while variations in logging policy are separated into different classes which implement the TEMPLATE METHOD. Clients of the framework select their logging policy by choosing which subclass to instantiate. Some users will want to use the standard logging options, while others may define their own custom logging, so you ensure the framework provides predefined logging subclasses.

This clean separation supports the understandability (Q1), maintainability (Q2), and evolvability (Q3) of both the framework and any additional logging policy classes introduced as part of concrete deployments.

Turn to 5.

Fig. 2. Step 8 - An unexpected null pointer exception may leave a system in an inconsistent state, causing an online shopping system to send an order to the wrong person. Illustration ©2008 Maisie Platts. E-mail: info@maisieplatts.com; WWW home page: http://maisieplatts.com/

Step 8

You decide to branch explicitly whenever a null logging STRATEGY object reference is detected within the COMMAND PROCESSOR. Unfortunately this introduces a great deal of repetition and complexity into the class, reducing understandability (Q1) and maintainability (Q2) of the framework code. A knock-on effect of this may even be a reduction in system reliability, if, for example, checks for null object references are forgotten.

See figure 2 for a real world example of the consequences of your decision.

Turn to 5.

Step 9

You decide to support compound requests through concrete COMMAND objects which aggregate other COMMAND objects. You don't need to make any changes to the existing framework because this type of functionality is already supported. But while this decision means the request handling framework itself is simpler, supporting understandability (Q1) and maintainability (Q2) of framework code, it means that clients of the framework will find it harder to use. Clients will need to represent each different compound request via a unique concrete class, which will be difficult to maintain (Q2), and harder to evolve (Q3).

Turn to 10.

Step 10

Congratulations, your request handling framework is complete! You've introduced an optional logging policy mechanism and support for compound requests. But is it easy to use, and is it easy to maintain? Is it everything you'd hoped for? The decisions were yours, so whatever they were, you now have to deal with the consequences!

The End

6   Analysis

Below, the features of the interactive story are discussed, and different paths through the story are compared. The benefits and liabilities of the approach are then examined, along with related and future work.

6.1   Interactive Story Features

Alternative Decision Points. At step 2 of the story the reader is presented with design alternatives that allow the choice of differing but equally desirable solutions to the problem - one choice leads to TEMPLATE METHOD, ther other to STRATEGY, both reasonable solutions given the context.

Optimal versus Sub-optimal Decision Points. The story also allows the reader to explore the negative consequences that may be encountered if the desirable solution for the context (i.e. the pattern) is not selected. For example at Step 3, the reader either opts for a transparent solution which leads to NULL OBJECT, or to introduce complicated control flow to deal with a missing STRATEGY.

Simple Decision Descriptions. The decision descriptions are intentionally brief, omitting many important details. The intention of this approach is to encourage the reader to explore all possible paths; decision texts provide just enough information to make a choice, but not enough that the 'right' choice is immediately obvious. Similarly, patterns are described through the story, but it is left to the reader to learn more through the thumbnails in the appendix, and associated references.

Joining Branches. The interactive story branches, but rejoins at steps 5 and 10. This demonstrates that not all branches in the story are irreconcilable. The story can be rejoined at these two points because the context of the remaining story is unaffected by differences introduced by the branches. Specifically, the choice of how to support compound requests at step 5 is unaffected by the choice of logging policy mechanism that was made previously. Note, however, that it may not always be possible to reconcile story branches.

Story Ending. Step 10 concludes the story by summarising the functional requirements the reader fulfilled, and by prompting the reader to assess their design. The ending is intentionally vague and unrelated to the design choices taken; this is because the consequences of each decision are described along the way. As such the ending could be either desirable or undesirable, and this depends on the consequences the reader has built up as they have gone. An alternative would be to present different endings depending on the reader's choices (see Further Work, below).

Illustrations. The story also includes an illustration associated with a particular story step. This acts to tie the reader's decisions to real world consequences, illustrating possible consequences of the reader's choices, and engaging the reader.

6.2   Comparison of Alternative Paths

To understand the interactive nature of the story, consider the following paths:

Route 1,2,3,4,5,6,10. The reader selects a delegation approach to introducing logging policy (i.e. STRATEGY), a transparent mechanism for handling a missing logging policies (i.e. NULL OBJECT), and a special COMMAND object for handling compound requests (i.e. COMPOSITE COMMAND).

Route 1,2,3,8,5,9,10. The reader selects a delegation approach to introducing logging policy (i.e. STRATEGY), but chooses to introduce special control flow handling for missing STRATEGY objects, and to ignore special handling of compound requests.

Comparison. The difference between the two routes is that the former route takes all possible optimal choices, while the latter takes all possible sub-optimal choices. In both cases, the choice of STRATEGY is a neutral choice because the alternative was equally viable.

This highlights the purpose of the story - to encourage the reader to learn about design by through exploration.

6.3   Benefits and Liabilities

Benefits. As mentioned above, benefits of the approach are that readers: have ability to explore different solutions to design problems; can experience both positive and negative consequences of design choices; will be engaged through the game-like format.

The decision making mechanism allows readers to explore various pattern-based designs possible for a particular set of requirements, and to experience negative consequences of sub-optimal choices. Going down the 'wrong' path gives the reader an understanding of negative consequences, but with no risk. Cheating is to be encouraged - after going down the wrong path, the reader can backtrack and change their mind, exposing them to the positive consequences of other choices. Subsequent readings of significantly different routes, such as those relating 'horror story' designs, may give the reader further insight.

Simple decision descriptions that omit information supporting reader choices, such as which choice is optimal, benefit the reader by encouraging the exploration of both optimal and sub-optimal paths. This encourages the reader to think 'outside the box', widening their exposure to all possible design consequences. However this approach may not always be appropriate because some readers may feel the game is 'rigged'. Similarly the omission of complete pattern descriptions may be confusing to some readers. A solution to both these problems is to ensure the reader is well-equipped with references to supporting material before they begin, along with guidance on how to approach making decisions and how to absorb the story.

Where interactive story paths are derived from a pattern language, the reader will gain an understanding of the overall context, problems and solutions, and pattern relationships in the language.

The format is engaging because reader decisions affect the outcome. The story takes on a game-like element where the set of outcomes is constrained by the reader's choices, providing an engaging, fun experience.

Further, interactive stories in the "Choose Your Own Adventure" format are written in a second person, genderless way. This avoids the dry, uninteresting tone of 'third person passive' writing. The authors of *"Pattern-Oriented Software Architecture: Volume 5"* [11] advise that *"A pattern description that is hard to read, passive to the point of comatose, formal, and aloof is likely to disengage the reader"* - a story written about YOU is much more engaging. Illustrations that show real world consequences of the reader's actions (as found in most children's interactive fiction) further engage the reader.

Liabilities. The main liability of the approach is the complexity of the writing task. Even writing the simple story above was non-trivial, requiring many different possibilities to be considered and accounted for. Interactive pattern stories are also difficult to modify after creation.

The complexity of the writing task suggests the approach is better suited to academic and educational fields than industrial projects, though starting with the pattern story from [11] and the pattern language in [7] simplified the writing process considerably. Tooling may also increase the feasibility of the approach, for example the Storyspace[3] or iWriter[4] tools may simplify story development.

The decisions in the example story also lack any choices around whether to fulfil requirements or not. Educational use of interactive pattern stories may require both design alternative and requirement fulfilment choices.

Another liability is that individual patterns or full designs from an interactive pattern story could be naively applied in an unsuitable context. For example the consequences of applying NULL OBJECT versus conditional null checking would be different if performance was a priority rather than understandability or maintainability. Such misapplication could lead to unexpected and undesirable consequences.

Finally, an interactive pattern story could be applied in a prescriptive way to limit design options, for example to force designers to always use STRATEGY to support transparent logging policies. This is likely to be unwelcome and would be considered a 'strait-jacket', unnecessarily restricting design choices.

6.4   Applicability

By extension from their non-interactive counterparts, interactive pattern stories are likely to be most useful for education and learning. The ability to explore a constrained design space in a fun, engaging way suggests that interactive pattern stories will be a useful addition to teaching and learning environments.

Different audiences may benefit in different (and multiple) ways from reading interactive pattern stories, so there are potentially as many applications as target audiences. By varying the content, choices, or emphasis, different aspects of software design and development may be illuminated.

The addition of explicit back-tracking options may be useful for certain audiences, for example where the writer wishes to ensure the reader will reach a certain story path (optimal or otherwise). The addition of code or UML model fragments and the creative use of typesetting such as italicising topic sentences may support educational applications further.

Interactive pattern stories may also serve as the basis of linear narrative stories, which may be desirable for some readers. Interactive stories written with

---

[3] Storyspace website: `http://www.eastgate.com/Storyspace.html`

[4] iWriter, by talkingpanda software: `http://talkingpanda.com/iwriter/`

tooling support would be suitable candidates for generating such linear stories, as long as tooling supported such functionality.

It may also be possible to employ the approach for software architecture evaluation and comparison. Where patterns are applied to create a software system, a pattern story may be written to capture the design choices made. It would then be possible to introduce alternative steps to describe other potential outcomes, for example a poor design choice that was avoided or a better design choice that was missed. Such an approach may prove useful in describing architecture rationale in an engaging way.

The approach is not thought to be well suited to industrial application or technical documentation because of the effort involved in creating and updating the stories. Again, tool support may make such applications feasible.

6.5 Related Work

Patterns, pattern languages, pattern sequences, and pattern stories can all be used for software design education, and are related to interactive pattern stories as follows.

Patterns provide examples of good solutions to design problems, study of which provides readers with an understanding of principles behind the good solution, and exemplary solutions which can serve as the basis of future designs [10]. Patterns provide the problems and good solutions for 'optimal' interactive story steps, suggest less optimal story steps that may occur if a pattern is not applied, and serve as the underlying descriptions of good design choices.

Pattern languages connect individual patterns together to form a broader guidance framework targetting a particular problem domain. The study of pattern languages provides an understanding of problems that occur in that domain, the patterns to apply to solve those problems, and how patterns are related [11]. Pattern languages can provide the overarching context for interactive stories, suggest potential story directions following story steps that describe applying a pattern, and provide underyling pattern descriptions targetting a particular domain.

Pattern sequences describe particular paths through a pattern language; a sequence describes a combination of patterns, solving related problems in a particular domain, which are known to have successfully created a good design for that domain [4]. Pattern sequences provide complete, optimal, story paths for an interactive pattern story, which must be filled in with details and augmented with alternatives to create a full interactive story.

Finally pattern stories provide concrete examples of one or more patterns in action [4]. A pattern story may be derived from a pattern sequence, or may simply tell the story of several patterns that were applied together to solve related design problems. The study of pattern stories allows readers to understand the concrete application of one or more patterns in the real world, filling in the gaps in the more abstract patterns, languages, and sequences. Pattern stories may used as the basis of interactive pattern stories, as is the case for the interactive story above.

The interactive pattern story concept builds on the pattern concept, may be applied in support of pattern languages and sequences, and is closely related to the pattern story concept. The key differences between pattern stories and their interactive form are: reader choices; the potential inclusion of sub-optimal design descriptions; and the engaging, educational format provided by interactive fiction.

6.6   Further Work

The biggest challenge to the successful application of interactive pattern stories is in authoring. The example presented above is simple enough to illustrate the benefits of interactive pattern stories; but stories developed for real-world use are likely to be more complex, and this carries a risk for writers in being overwhelmed by complexity. In particular the introduction of multiple endings is known to be problematic, requiring overlapping narrative in different story steps, and occasionally artificial design choices to provide complete coverage of all options. Further work is required to find a simple, accessible story format and structure that avoids accidentally complexity, allows exploration of design choices, and keeps the writer focussed on the story rather than the mechanisms of its telling.

A second area of further work is to test interactive pattern stories in the real world. While an informal workshop at ACCU 2009[5] supports the benefits outlined here, a more formal study is needed. The creation and application of one or more interactive pattern stories with a group of student volunteers is one option.

Other areas of exploration are the application of tool based approaches to both story writing and telling, and the use of other media such as board games or card based games (e.g. STRATEGY trumps TEMPLATE METHOD[6]).

7   Conclusions

This paper proposed the introduction of interactivity into pattern stories to engage readers and support the exploration of pattern-based designs and pattern languages for educational purposes. The *"Choose Your Own Adventure"* game-book format was proposed as a suitable basis for introducing interactivity.

An example interactive story was used to show the benefits of the proposed medium to software design education. In the story, the reader was able to explore design alternatives in solving a fixed set of functional requirements, where consequences were described in relation to several quality requirements.

The benefits of the approach are that readers can explore different solutions to design problems, that readers can experience both positive and negative consequences of design choices, and that the reader is engaged by the game-like format. The liabilities are the complexity of the writing task, the possibility of pattern

---

[5] Workshop on "Exploring Design Space with interactive pattern stories", James Siddle and Kevlin Henney, ACCU 2009.

[6] Top Trumps official website: http://www.toptrumps.com/

misapplication, and the fact that prescriptive stories may be unwelcome. The approach was considered to be applicable primarily in educational environments.

Further work is needed to find a simple, accessible story format that shields the writer from complexity but provides readers with the ability to explore design choices and consequences.

Acknowledgements

Thanks to Paris Avgeriou for providing many insights and useful feedback during the shepherding of this paper for EuroPLoP 2008, and to Kevlin Henney for providing feedback on an early version of the paper. Thanks also to the authors of POSA volumes 4 and 5 and to John Wiley & Sons Ltd for granting permission to use the request handling framework story, and to Maisie Platts for providing permission to use her illustration. Thank you also to Sam Clark of Thames Hudson for providing excellent feedback and guidance on the layout of the paper. Thanks to Oxford University's Kellogg college for providing funding for me to attend EuroPLoP 2008. Finally thank you to the reviewers and editors of Transactions on Pattern Languages of Programs for supporting the development of the final version of this paper.

References

1. Jackson, S., Livingstone, I.: The Warlock of Firetop Mountain, 25th Anniversary edn. Wizard Books (August 2007)
2. Packard, E.: Choose Your Own Adventure 1: The Cave of Time. Bantam Books (1979)
3. Alexander, C., Ishikawa, S., Silverstein, M.: A Pattern Language: Towns, Buildings, Construction. Oxford University Press, Oxford (1997)
4. Henney, K.: Context Encapsulation. Three Stories, a Language, and Some Sequences. In: EuroPLoP Conference Proceedings (2005)
5. Montfort, N.: Twisty Little Passages: An Approach to Interactive Fiction. MIT Press, Cambridge (2004)
6. Buschmann, F., Henney, K., Schmidt, D.C.: 7. Pattern Sequences. In: Pattern-Oriented Software Architecture. On Patterns and Pattern Languages, vol. 5, pp. 186–188. John Wiley and Sons, Chichester (2007)
7. Buschmann, F., Henney, K., Schmidt, D.C.: Pattern-Oriented Software Architecture. A Pattern Language for Distributed Computing, vol. 4. John Wiley and Sons, Chichester (2007)
8. Buschmann, F., Henney, K., Schmidt, D.C.: 9. Elements of Language. In: Pattern-Oriented Software Architecture. On Patterns and Pattern Languages, vol. 5, pp. 251–254. John Wiley and Sons, Chichester (2007)
9. Bass, L., Clements, P., Kazman, R.: Software Architecture in Practice, 2nd edn. Addison Wesley, Reading (2003)
10. Gamma, E., Helm, R., Johnson, R., Vlissides, J.: Design Patterns - Elements of Reusable Object-Oriented Software. Addison-Wesley, Reading (1995)
11. Buschmann, F., Henney, K., Schmidt, D.C.: Pattern-Oriented Software Architecture. On Patterns and Pattern Languages, vol. 5. John Wiley and Sons, Chichester (2007)
12. Martin, R.C., Riehle, D., Buschmann, F. (eds.): Pattern Languages of Program Design, vol. 3. Addison-Wesley Longman Publishing Co., Inc., Boston (1997)

Appendices

Appendix - Pattern Thumbnails

For the purposes of this paper the patterns used in the interactive story are paraphrased below, with references to suitable pattern descriptions:

Collections For States. [7] For objects that need to be operated on collectively with regard to their current state, represent each state of interest by a separate collection that refers to all objects in that state.

Command. [10] When decoupling the sender of a request from its receiver, encapsulate requests being made into command objects. Provide these command objects with a common interface to execute the requests that they represent.

Command Processor. [7] When an application can receive requests from multiple clients, provide a command processor to execute requests on client's behalf within the constraints of the application.

Composite Command. [11] When a transparent and simple mechanism for single and compound request execution is needed, express requests as COMMANDs, and group multiple COMMANDs in a COMPOSITE to ensure that single and multiple requests are treated uniformly.

Explicit Interface. [7] To enable component reuse, whilst avoiding unnecessary coupling to component internals, separate the declared interface of a component from its implementation.

Memento. [10] To enable the recording of an object's internal state without breaking encapsulation, snapshot and encapsulate the relevant state within a separate memento object. Pass this memento to the object's clients rather than providing direct access to internal state.

Null Object. [12] If some object behaviour will only execute when a particular object exists, create and use a null object instead of checking for null object references. This avoids the unnecessary introduction of complex and repetitious null checking.

Strategy. [10] Where an object has a common core, but may vary in some behavioural aspects, capture the varying behavioural aspects in a set of strategy classes, plug in an appropriate instance, then delegate execution of the variant behaviour to the appropriate strategy object.

Template Method. [10] Where an object has a common core, but may vary in some behavioural aspects, create a superclass that expresses the common behavioural core then delegate execution of behavioural variants to hook methods that are overridden by subclasses.

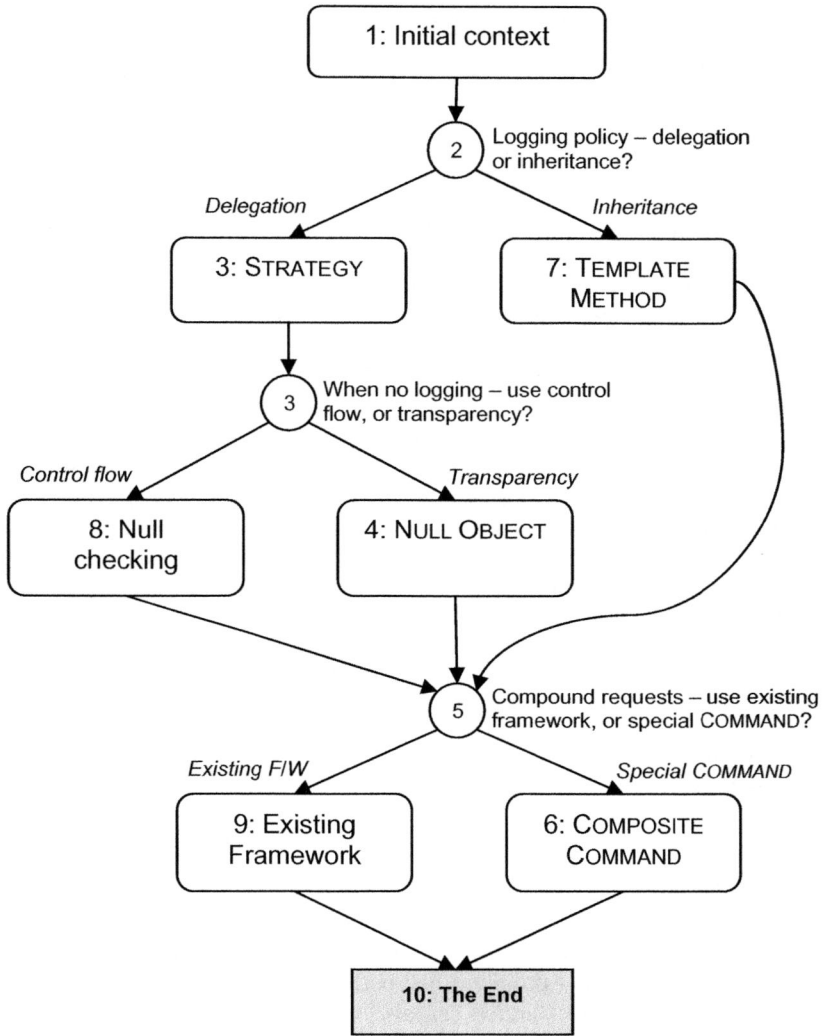

Fig. 3. Map of Story 1 - Varying Design Choices

Appendix - Story Map

Figure 3 provides an overview of the decisions that you can make and the different routes through the interactive story found in this paper.

Circles represent decisions points and italicised text shows possible choices; rounded boxes represent the resulting development activities and decision consequences; numbers denote discrete steps in the interactive story. Where the numbered steps describe both development activities and choices, the numbers are repeated in the diagram. The grey box represents text that summarises the story at the end.

Experiences in Using Patterns to Support Process Experts in Process Description and Wizard Creation

Birgit Zimmermann[1], Christoph Rensing[2], and Ralf Steinmetz[2]

[1] SAP AG, SAP Research Center Darmstadt Bleichstr. 8, 64283 Darmstadt, Germany
birgit.zimmermann@sap.com
[2] KOM Multimedia Communications Lab, Technische Universität Darmstadt,
Merckstr. 25, 64283 Darmstadt, Germany
{christoph.rensing,ralf.steinmetz}@kom.tu-darmstadt.de

Abstract. The adaptation of existing E-Learning material to a changed usage scenario is a complex task. But in reality, often the persons, who have to adapt existing material, are not experts in performing all needed tasks. Thus, to be able to support those persons, it would be desirable to provide a tool based on expert knowledge about how to perform the processes. In this paper an approach is presented, how experts in performing adaptation processes can provide their knowledge about the processes via a pattern based description formalism. A wizard guiding users step by step through the described adaptation processes can be derived from the patterns. This wizard offers expert knowledge to persons who are novices in performing adaptation processes.

Keywords: Process description, Process support, Patterns, E-Learning, Adaptation, Reuse.

1 Overview

Users of software often complain that many software solutions only insufficiently support them in solving their problems and performing their tasks. This phenomenon occurs with all kinds of software. It can also be seen with tools that are especially developed to support users in performing specific tasks. Working on a tool supporting users in performing so called adaptation processes we found the same problem.

Adaptation processes are needed to adapt existing E-Learning material in order to make it suited for changed usage scenarios. There exist lots of different kinds of such adaptation processes (e.g. adaptations to a changed corporate design, terminological adaptations, or content translation) [19]. Thus several aspects have to be considered (layout, didactics, linguistics, technology). In addition various different formats are used (such as HTML, PPT or Flash), often within one course. Unfortunately, many authors, who have to adapt E-Learning material, do not have the knowledge to perform all the adaptations needed. Therefore a tool offering support to authors in performing E-Learning material adaptations would be useful. To offer tool support for adaptation processes we created a wizard based on a pattern based description formalism for adaptation processes. This paper presents our experiences with this approach. The next chapter gives an introduction to adaptation processes.

J. Noble et al. (Eds.): TPLOP II, LNCS 6510, pp. 34–61, 2011.

2 An Introduction to the Example Scenario: Adaptation Processes

Creating high-quality E-Learning material is a time and cost consuming task. Re-using existing material could reduce these costs. But often a one-to-one reuse of the existing material is not possible, as the new scenario of usage differs to a certain degree from the original usage scenario. Therefore, to achieve a high quality, it is necessary to adapt the existing material to the new usage scenario. There exist a lot of different adaptations. [19, 20] give an overview of those adaptations.

The processes needed to perform the adaptations are structured hierarchically: A process is performed by executing several process steps. These process steps can consist of smaller process steps or of atomic operations that cannot be split up into smaller units (see figure 1).

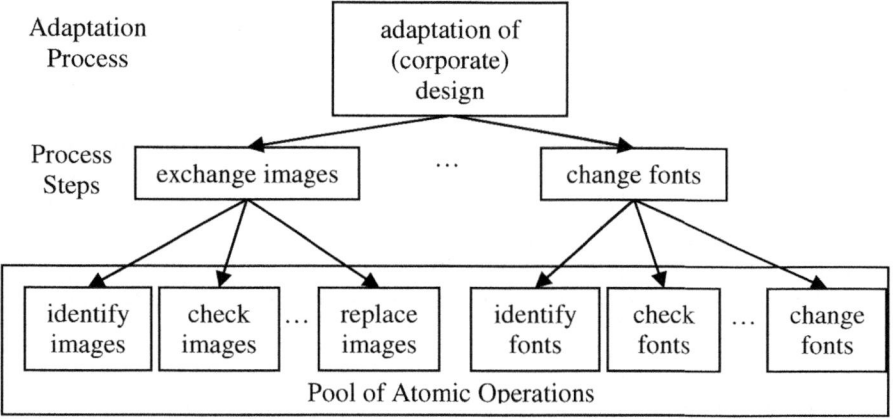

Fig. 1. Process hierarchy

Let us have a look at one example process: The adaptation of E-Learning material to a changed (corporate) design consists of several process steps like exchanging logos and images that do not fit, or changing fonts, backgrounds, colors, etc. The process step "exchanging images" consists of several atomic operations like identifying all used images, testing for each image, if it fits to the requirements, finding images that have to be used instead of non-fitting images etc.

Some of the adaptations are quite complex. Translating text in a text box, for example, can change the length of the text. Then it has to be decided if the text box has to be enlarged, or if the text has to be shortened, or if this fact does not matter. Someone, who is not working as a translator, might not be aware of all these possibilities.

In addition, in many cases it is necessary to perform several adaptations in order to achieve a good result. When a course that has been produced for one company has to be reused in another company, the layout has to fit the new corporate design. In addition it is often also needed to change the terminology, in order to adapt it to the terminology of the new company.

But in reality, often the persons, who have to adapt the material, are not experts in performing all needed tasks. Mostly they only have a certain basic knowledge of how to perform the adaptation processes. This means that compared to Dreyfus' model of skills [3] they are novices in performing adaptation processes. But with the help of a tool that is based on the knowledge of persons from the expert level it is possible that the novices are supported in performing adaptation processes in such a way that they are enabled to achieve results that a user from a higher skill level would achieve. To develop such a tool support was our goal within the Content Sharing Project (http://www.contentsharing.com).

To be able to offer support for adaptation processes it was necessary to find out how the adaptation processes have to be performed and how a useful tool support could look like. Therefore we carried out a survey of persons being experts in performing the processes needed to adapt existing E-Learning material in order to make it suited for changed usage scenarios [19]. These persons perform adaptation processes very often. Therefore they can offer a detailed description of how to perform the processes.

Many of the adaptation process experts mentioned that existing tools are not well suited to support users in performing the adaptation processes. Especially novice users are often not able to use these tools. The main reason for this problem is that the tools often do not represent the processes themselves. They are based on the software designers understanding of the processes [10]. But in many cases this understanding differs from the processes as they are performed and understood by the process experts [12]. Thus we decided to look for a possibility that allows adaptation process experts to be involved more directly in the development of a tool offering support for adaptation processes.

3   Problem: How to Enable Process Experts to Describe Adaptation Processes?

Traditional software development often starts with analysis activities in order to collect information about how processes are performed. The requirements from user side as well as from system side are collected. Based on these requirements, models of the processes are developed and implemented [13]. The exact proceeding can deviate depending on the underlying project structure (e.g. software development according to v-model, spiral models, extreme programming, rational unified process etc.).

But this proceeding often leads to problems caused by misunderstandings between process experts and software designers and developers [12]. To make things worse, it is often not possible for process experts to control if the models really describe their processes, as they do not have knowledge of common modelling formalisms like UML or ARIS. According to Siau et al. [17] UML is too complex in many cases and its constructs are ambiguous. The same holds for ARIS [14].

Someone, who for example is working as a translator (an adaptation that occurs very often), is a process expert for translation. Normally this person is not simultaneously an experienced software developer or designer. Therefore most translators are not able to deal with common modelling formalisms as UML, ARIS or BPMN [1], as they do not need these methods in their daily work. The same holds for many other adaptation processes: Mostly persons have expertise in the processes they deal with in their daily work. Thus they are able to give a detailed description of how they perform these processes. But many of these persons have never learned to describe their processes with common modelling formalisms.

Thus, in order to integrate adaptation process experts more closely into the development of a tool supporting the adaptation of existing E-Learning material, it would be desirable to facilitate adaptation process experts to describe their process knowledge in a way that is easy to understand and that does not require extensive training. This knowledge should be used for software creation. To be able to solve this problem it was necessary to find a possibility that fulfils the following requirements:

- In order to enable the process experts to describe adaptation processes on their own, the process description formalism has to be easy to understand and easy to learn.
- In order to be able to get an understanding of a possible tool support a prototypic support tool should be created based on the process descriptions provided by the process experts. This prototype should give process experts a possibility to find out if a given process description is correctly reflected in the prototype and if a tool based on the prototype would support the described adaptation process in the desired way.
- At the same time it has to be considered that the description formalism has to be structured in such a way that on one hand it is possible to create the prototype mentioned above based on the description in a way that does not require development skills. On the other hand, the prototype has to solve as a basis for further development. This means that the prototype as well as the process description have to contain all information needed to create a prototype and to allow a developer to implement a computer program by enhancing the prototype.

For the adaptation process expert it is important that the description formalism can be used without extensive training. For the developer it is important that the description formalism allows using familiar software development proceedings and tools as far as possible. We wanted to find an approach that meets both requirements. This approach should be used to enhance the software development processes existing by now. It was not intended to replace those processes.

4   Solution: Pattern Based Wizard Creation

4.1   Using Patterns to Describe Adaptation Processes

As described before it was our aim to find an approach to integrate the adaptation experts more directly into the creation of a tool that supports novices in executing adaptation processes. Such a tool should be based on process descriptions provided by process experts. In order to be manageable by adaptation process experts, the formalism, used to write down the process descriptions, has to satisfy a number of requirements:

- The description formalism must be easy to understand without specific previous knowledge, as most process experts are not familiar with common methods used in software development to describe processes.
- The process descriptions have to enable persons, who are not adaptation process experts, to perform the adaptation processes in a satisfying way.
- Based on the process descriptions a prototype should be created that serves as a basis for further development. Thus, software designers as well as software developers should be able to use the descriptions as basis for developing software programs in a way they are used to.

As stated before, classical software development often leads to misunderstandings between process experts and software designers and developers. Thus we decided to offer a prototype as a common basis for communication between those parties. In order to make sure that the prototype reflects the process experts' understanding of the processes we were searching for a possibility that allows process experts to develop a prototype on their own that is based on their process descriptions. This leads to some additional requirements for the process description formalism for adaptation processes:

- The description of an adaptation process has to contain all information needed to create a prototype.
- As the prototype creation should be done in an automated way (compare next section), the process description must be stored in a form that makes automated prototype creation possible.

We decided to use patterns to capture the process knowledge of adaptation experts and to store these patterns in an XML format. Patterns document proven solutions to recurring problems; they describe best practices [7]. Patterns are noted in natural language. Hence they are easy to understand for the persons of whom knowledge is collected with the patterns [6].

Patterns offer a regular form and they can have a structured, fixed notation. They can be stored in an XML format like the Pattern Language Markup Language (PLML) [11]. (PLML is an XML DTD, which originally was thought of as a common standard for HCI patterns). XML is very flexible. It offers the possibility to be used for several different areas of application. For example, XML can be rendered to HTML or other formats, e.g. by using XSLT. In this way it is readable for a non IT person. At the same time it is very structured and thus machine readable. Besides it can be imported to established UML modelling tools by using XML Metadata Interchange (XMI).

Patterns are written down in natural language. Therefore pattern based process descriptions are easy to understand for adaptation process experts. In addition software designers as well as developers will find their familiar views on pattern based process descriptions stored in XML, because of the flexibility of XML.

But most process experts are not able to generate XML files. Therefore we developed a two-stage proceeding for the creation of process descriptions: First the knowledge of process experts had to be captured in an easy to understand, pattern based format. In a second step this format had to be mapped to a formal XML representation allowing to generate a prototype based on the given information.

Note that patterns are not processes: In our approach we used patterns to describe how a certain process that solves a recurring problem can be performed. Thus, these patterns describe (parts of) processes needed to adapt existing E-Learning material on a high level. They contain important information about how to proceed. Especially they contain a section naming all needed process steps. Some other pattern formats also include sections describing concrete steps in detail. But as process steps are sometimes needed in several processes, we name the steps and – if needed – their order within a pattern. But we separate their concrete description from the patterns. We added a second kind of descriptions for the process steps, which we called how-to guides. These how-to guides explain in detail, what has to be done, to perform each process step and which smaller process steps or atomic operations are needed during the execution of a process step. Compared to the patterns describing the whole process the how-to guides are much more detailed.

Atomic operations are process steps, which cannot be split up into smaller units. Most atomic operations are used in several process steps. Therefore we also have separately written down instructions for all atomic operations needed in the process steps.

4.2 Wizards for Process Support

Wizards are a common solution in computer science, to offer users without expert knowledge a step by step guidance through processes. According to [5] wizards can be used, if novices have to perform a complex task composed of several steps. The novices know which goals they want to reach, but they do not necessarily know which steps they have to perform to reach the goal. A wizard helps them in reaching their goals.

Wizards are easy to use even for users, who are not familiar with the processes supported by the wizard. Adaptation processes often have to be carried out by persons who are not experts in performing these processes. Therefore they need detailed step by step guidance through the adaptation processes. Thus we decided to develop a wizard as a supporting tool for this kind of processes.

As stated before, it was our aim to enable the process experts to be involved more directly into the software creation process in order to achieve software that is based on their knowledge. Thus we were searching for a possibility allowing the process experts to prove the outcome of their process descriptions. But adaptation process experts often have no knowledge of common modelling formalisms. And we did not want them to be forced to learn common modelling formalisms or programming techniques. We therefore decided to develop a method that allows process experts to generate a prototypic wizard, which is based on the process descriptions written by the process experts. With the prototype it can be checked, whether the underlying process descriptions really describe how the processes are performed. As most of the experts in performing adaptation processes do not have the knowledge to develop such a wizard, the wizard development method should be easy to use for persons without programming experience. Therefore we wanted an automated wizard generation that does not require expertise in software development. To be manageable for process experts and to be a useful basis for further development, the wizard as well as its generation have to meet certain requirements:

- The wizard should be based on the process descriptions written down in the pattern based notation formalism (described in section 4.1), as they contain all information needed to carry out the processes.
- To be able to offer process guidance for novices the wizard has to describe, how to perform the adaptation processes step by step.
- The generation of the wizard should be done in an automated way that can be managed by the adaptation process expert.
- The generation has to be done quickly, as the process experts might perform the following circle several times: write process description - create prototypic wizard - check wizard - if the wizard does not fully meet the expectations: adapt process description - generate revised wizard - etc.
- The generated prototypic wizard should be extendable by automated functionalities. Thus a developer could create a supporting tool for adaptation processes based on the wizard generated by the adaptation process experts.

We developed a wizard generation tool that meets these requirements. The tool is described in section 6.

4.3 Implementation

In this section we give an introduction of the implementation of our approach. Section 5, 6, and 7 offer a detailed description.

As stated in section 4.1, the patterns, process step descriptions and atomic operations descriptions contain the knowledge of the adaptation process experts. To be able to create a prototypic wizard out of these process descriptions we needed a structured, machine readable representation of this information. Because of its flexibility we have chosen an XML notation (adapted from PLML) to store the patterns describing the adaptation processes (compare section 4.1). We also used XML to store the process step descriptions and the atomic step descriptions.

But most process experts have no or only limited knowledge of XML. Because of this we developed a process description input tool (PIT), which supports users in writing down pattern like process descriptions and saving them as XML files. PIT stores the descriptions given by the process experts in two files: one file containing all textual information about the process and a second file containing a graph representation of the structure of the process. This proceeding corresponds to the two-stage proceeding for the creation of process descriptions mentioned before (section 4.1):

1. In a first step PIT allows to capture the process knowledge in an easy to understand format. This is done with a pattern based description formalism. The pattern based process descriptions can be created with the help of the tool PIT.
2. In a second step PIT maps the format to a formal XML representation that allows to generate a prototypic wizard based on the information provided in the process description.

As described in section 4.2, a prototypic wizard, generated based on the process descriptions, can offer process experts the possibility to check if an adaptation process is reflected correctly. For this purpose we developed the wizard generation tool (WGT).

WGT takes the XML files as input. It then generates a wizard by interpreting the data provided by PIT. The generated wizard represents a first prototype of a process support wizard. It can be taken as a common ground for communication between IT experts and process experts. In addition it can serve as a starting point for further development done by experienced software developers.

Thus the pattern-based wizard generation approach proposed in this paper is based on a three-step proceeding:

1. Writing pattern like process descriptions and store them in XML
2. Automated wizard generation
3. Extension of prototypic wizard

Each of these steps is explained in detail in the next sections.

5   Step 1: Writing Process Descriptions

In the first step the process expert has to create a pattern like process description. For each process one pattern is created that describes the process in general: What problem is solved by the process? Which things have to be kept in mind? If a process is more complicated and contains several sub-processes, it is possible to create patterns for the sub-processes and to link them to the super process. (This is realized via a specific type of related patterns.)

The patterns describe the process on a high level, as they explain how the process helps to solve a certain problem. But to perform the process one has to know which process steps and atomic operations have to be performed and how this has to be done. Thus, in addition to the high level process description, the process step descriptions and the descriptions of the atomic operations have to be created.

To support process experts in creating process descriptions in the needed format the process description input tool (PIT) has been created. PIT is a Java application developed under Eclipse. It offers an input form helping process experts to describe processes in the required pattern based notation formalism.

Figure 10 in the appendix presents a part of PIT's input form for process descriptions. One can see that the process description contains common pattern elements like intent, context, or problem statement. These elements provide a reason why a process can be applied, why a certain context has to be fulfilled to be able to perform the process etc. Thus they are useful for other persons who might want to perform the described process. All this information is very valuable to all persons, who have to decide, which process helps them in solving a specific problem, and who are not process experts.

As shown in figure 10, mandatory input fields are marked with an asterisk. We have chosen these elements as mandatory as they are most important to other persons in order to understand why and how a process has to be performed. Mandatory elements are:

- The **pattern ID** is a unique ID used to address the pattern. It is created automatically.
- The **name** provides a first, rough idea what the pattern is about.
- The **problem** section describes the situation addressed by the pattern.
- The **solution** explains to the user, how the problem can be solved.
- The **process steps** list all steps needed to execute the solution.
- The **consequences** help other persons, to decide if they want to apply a pattern or not, depending on if the positive consequences are more important than the negative ones.

The non mandatory elements are needed, if a process expert wants to write a pattern, but they are not necessary, to offer a useful process description:

- The process expert has a certain **confidence** in the process description. (As we talk about process experts the confidence should be high.)
- The **intent** gives a short overview, what a pattern is about.
- The **context** describes the situation, where the pattern can occur.
- The process expert can give an **example** of a successful application of the pattern.
- The **forces** describe the sometimes contradicting trade-offs that must be considered when performing the process.
- **Known uses** describe situations, where the pattern has been applied successfully.
- **Related patterns** can exist, but it might be that there are no related patterns.

Note that the process descriptions we have collected for adaptation processes meet the quality criteria of being patterns (like being general, having at least three know uses, etc.). But the process descriptions written down by process experts need not to be patterns. If a process expert creates a process description with PIT, PIT ensures that all information needed to generate a prototypic wizard is given. But PIT does not check if the process description is a pattern. But also process descriptions that are no patterns offer valuable information and a good basis for wizard creation.

When the process expert stores a process description, the given information is stored in XML files. The XML files contain in one file the textual description of the process and in a separate file the graph representation defining the process flow and all its dependencies and preconditions. In the appendix a DTD of the XML file containing the process information can be found. Many of the elements of this DTD are taken from PLML [11]. The PLML v1.1 DTD contains some additional elements that have not been taken into account here: `alias`, `synopsis`, `diagram`, `rationale`, `literature`, `pattern-link` and `management`. The patterns taken as a starting point for this work do not need these elements.

But our patterns contain some elements that have a slightly different meaning compared to PLML. The PLML element `illustration` is called `example_illustration`, as to our understanding, this better explains what is meant by this element. To be able to better differentiate the `example` as used in PLML from the `example_illustration` we call it `example_explanation`. What is referenced as an `implementation` in PLML is called `process_steps` in our DTD. The `related_patterns` already contain a link to the pattern they are related to. Therefore our `related_patterns` are a kind of a combination between `related-patterns` and `pattern-link` in PLML.

The following elements that are used in our DTD are not mentioned in PLML, but they are necessary in our approach:

- `intent`: The intent explains what the pattern aims for.
- `known_uses`: The known uses are part of the example-section in PLML. In our patterns the example only contains one known-use. Other known uses can be added by using this element.
- `consequences`: The consequences occur when the pattern has been applied. Positive and negative consequences can occur. As for a reader of a pattern it is very important to know, what will happen when applying the pattern, we added this section.

5.1 Defining Process Steps and Atomic Operations

The steps of a process, their interdependencies, and the preconditions for the execution of each step constitute the process. Thus process steps are essential for the execution of a process. Also branching ("if step A leads to result A' then perform step B else perform step C") and cycles ("repeat step A until condition B is fulfilled") within the process flow are of importance. Hence PIT provides a special wizard to define the process steps. This wizard allows a fine granular specification of the process flow without requiring special knowledge of process modelling. It is started by pressing a button to add a step to the process description.

With this wizard users can define for each step, if the execution of a step is mandatory or optional, or if certain preconditions have to be fulfilled, before the step can be executed, or if there are dependencies on other steps. Branches are embodied by a special kind of precondition: If the precondition leads to one result, one step is executed, if it leads to another result, another step is executed. Cycles are defined by specifying a step that is the starting point for the cycle and another one, which is the end point. In addition a termination condition has to be defined. This is again modelled by a special kind of a precondition.

Figure 2 shows the screen used to define a step that has to be performed, if other steps have been performed before. Another part of the wizard helps users to define preconditions and a third one allows to model cycles. In addition an input form exists, used to describe how a process step has to be performed. The description of process steps is also stored in the process description file.

Compared to the pattern based description of a whole process, the process step description is very short: It contains the name of the process step, a detailed description of how to perform the process step and a listing of all smaller process steps and atomic operations needed when performing the process step. Sometimes a process step is as complex that it can be regarded as a complete process on its own. Then it is possible to create a process description for this step. This description can be added to the process step description via a special link. In the wizard this is presented as a link to an additional page containing the complex description. Users of the wizard can then read this additional information.

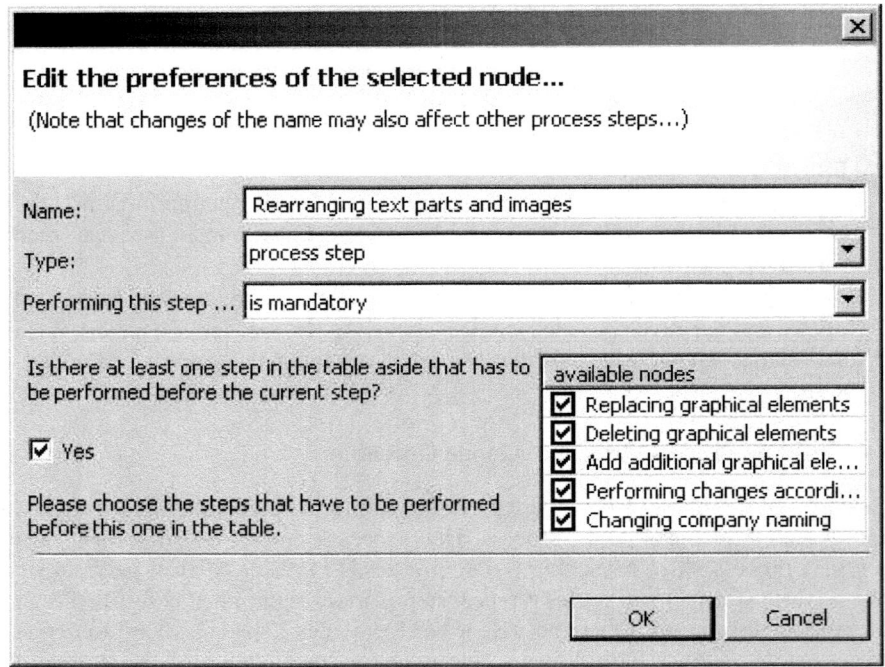

Fig. 2. Defining dependencies between steps

As steps themselves consist of smaller steps - atomic operations or again process steps - it is also possible to define all operations and smaller steps needed to perform a process step. Again a wizard helps to state if the execution is mandatory or optional, or if certain preconditions have to be fulfilled. Dependencies on other atomic operations can also be determined. For each atomic operation a description has to be provided, how the operation is executed. This can be done via a special input form.

There exist three different kinds of atomic operations: queries, decisions and executions.

- **Queries** are needed to determine information. For example: Find all images used in an E-Learning course.
- **Decisions** are needed if a person, who performs the process, has to decide on something. For example: Decide for each image, if the image has to be deleted or not.
- **Executions** are needed, whenever something is changed or done. For example: Delete all images that have been chosen for deletion.

Based on the information represented via the process steps and the atomic operations the second XML file is created. This file represents the process flow. It names all steps and atomic operations. For each step or atomic operation it contains the information whether the execution is mandatory or not, and if there exist preconditions or dependencies. Via the pattern ID, process step ID, and atomic operation ID it is possible to map the information stored in this file to the information stored in the description file. Listing 2 in the appendix contains an example for such a process graph description.

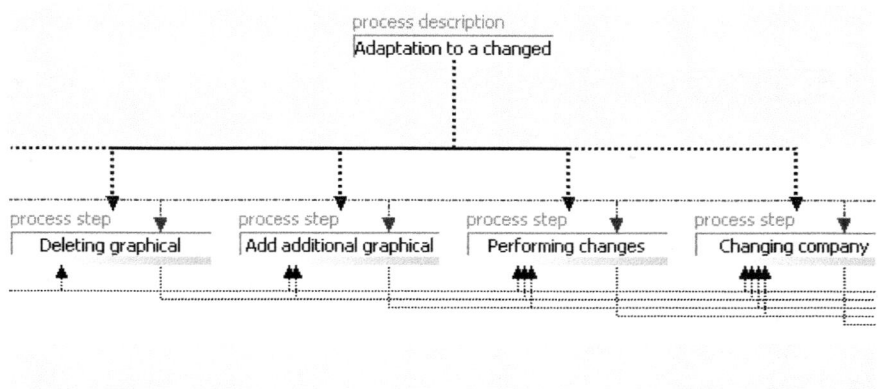

Fig. 3. Visualization of a process graph

PIT offers several possibilities to work with the generated process descriptions: It is certainly possible to edit an existing description. In addition the textual description stored in XML can be rendered as HTML in order to view it via a browser. Thereby it is possible to read the entire process description as a continuous text. Thus, it is more comfortable to control, whether the description is complete and accurate. Furthermore, a visualization of the process graph is available that represents all steps of the process flow. (Figure 3 shows the first level of the process graph corresponding to listing 2 in the appendix. By clicking on a process step the level under this step opens in the viewer.) At the moment this visualization is only a first prototype. Further enhancements are planned. As the process descriptions are stored in XML it is possible to offer several visualizations that are tailored to the needs of several persons (a developer and a process expert need, for example, different visualizations). In addition it is planned to offer an export to XMI. The XMI files could be used to provide a class diagram and an activity diagram representing the process.

6 Step 2: Automated Wizard Generation

The XML files generated by PIT serve as input for the wizard generation tool (WGT) used in step 2 of the proceeding proposed here. WGT is a Java application developed under Eclipse. Based on the information of PIT's XML files it generates a wizard that, as a first prototype, can be used as a starting point for further development.

WGT is started by selecting a menu entry in PIT. WGT reads the process description that is actually open within PIT. The user specifies where the generated wizard has to be stored and starts the wizard generation by simply pressing a button (compare figure 4). WGT then parses the XML files created by PIT. It extracts the information contained in the files and fills several predefined code templates with this information. By this procedure all needed Java classes for the prototype are created. The "Activate additional options..." section shown in figure 4 can be activated to open a dialog that allows to specify, how the atomic operations have to be distributed over the wizard pages. (Later in this chapter this is explained more detailed.)

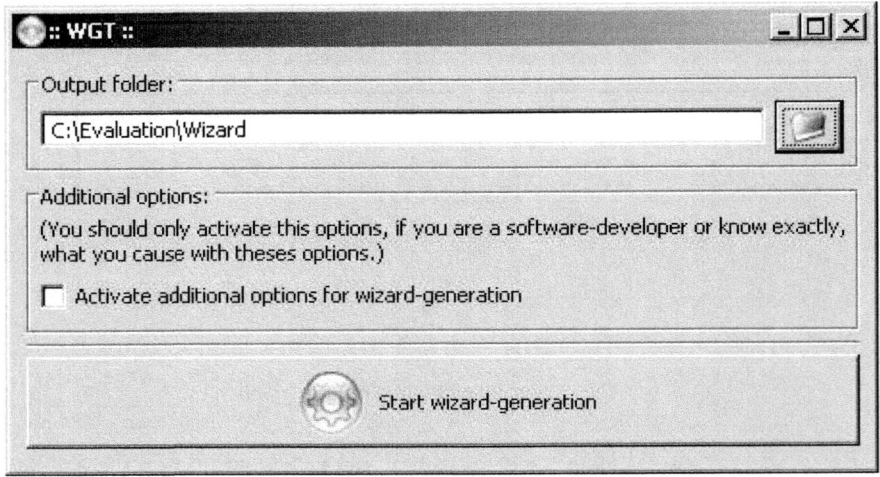

Fig. 4. Screenshot of WGT

The main purpose of the wizard generation tool is to generate a wizard based on the information given by the process descriptions created with PIT. Note that the process descriptions contain more information than a "normal" pattern: They contain the pattern like process description, the process step descriptions and the descriptions of all needed atomic operations. Thus, the wizard can provide all information needed to carry out a certain adaptation process.

The wizard has a graphical user interface, which allows directly after its generation that the process expert evaluates whether the wizard contains all needed information and whether the process flow is correct. The design of the user interface follows common rules for designing user interfaces, as described in [2, 15].

The atomic operations used in the wizard are not automated directly after generating the wizard. Instead the wizard contains descriptions telling a user, how to proceed. We believe that it leads to better results, if an experienced software developer checks, where it is reasonably possible to automate certain operations, compared to trying to automate functions already during wizard generation. Where this is possible the developer can extend the automatically generated source code. To make it easier for the developer, to find where the source code can be extended, comments are added to the automatically generated source code during its creation.

As stated before, another important point during wizard generation is the time needed to generate the wizard. As long as the wizard does not fulfil all needs, the process expert will change the description created with PIT and generate a new version of the wizard. Thus it is highly probable that the process expert will use WGT several times until a wizard is generated that really fulfils all needs. Therefore WGT has to be fast in order to reduce the time, where the process expert has to wait for the generation to finish.

As large parts of the source code stay the same, code generation templates exist for most wizard classes. There are several kinds of page templates and composite templates depending on the function of each part of the wizard: One template exists for the start page of the wizard, another one for the last page. A special page template exists for process steps. This template contains a part, where the description of the process step can be added. The atomic operations are realized via composites that are based on composite templates. For the three different types of atomic operations three different templates are used. The composites of the operations of a process step are grouped together on one page, which is also created based on a template. This allows a fast source code generation.

The wizard generation tool consists of three logical units that are passed one after the other (shown in figure 5):

1. In the first part the XML files provided by PIT are read. The information about the process flow is transferred into an internal process structure model and the information contained in the descriptions is extracted.
2. The second part uses this information to map it to Java code templates. The textual information is used to enhance the content of the graphical user interface. The structural information is used to create all process steps and to transfer the structure of the process flow to the wizard. By this all needed Java classes are generated.
3. The third part writes the generated source code to several Java classes and marks all parts in the source code that can be enhanced by adding additional source code. In addition the created classes are compiled and a batch file is created that allows starting the wizard comfortably.

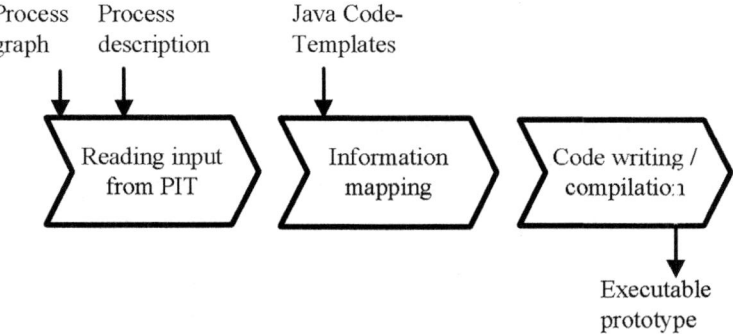

Fig. 5. Three phases of WGT

The prototype wizard generated by WGT is based on the model-view-controller principle [4]:

- The process graph containing information about the process flow serves as *model*.
- The wizard pages providing a graphical user interface build the *view*. Those pages contain the textual information of the pattern-based process description. They are based on Java code templates. WGT instantiates those templates by filling them with the given information. The pages then contain a detailed description on how to perform the process, each process step, and each atomic operation.
- The *controller* of the wizard passes events caused by the user to the model and reactions caused by the model back to the user. The controller interprets the process flow information provided by the model. Depending on the user input the controller monitors, which step has to be performed at which time and which step is possible as next step. Thus, the controller assures a correct process flow. In addition it contains information about the actual state of the wizard, as it stores, which steps have been carried out so far as well as their results. This is important for a further implementation of the wizard enhancing it with automated functionality. The controller also has to collect and distribute all data that have been created or are required when performing several steps in an automated way.

6.1   Arranging Steps and Operations on Pages

One problem when creating the wizard is how to distribute the process steps and atomic operations over the wizard pages. There are several possibilities, how to solve this problem: One could create one page explaining each process step and one additional page for each atomic operation. As many adaptations consist of quite a lot of process steps and atomic operations, this can easily lead to a huge number of pages with sometimes only a short explanation on it. Therefore we discarded this possibility.

Another possibility would be to create one page for each process step, and to add all atomic operations needed in the process step to this page. But many process steps contain ten and more atomic operations. Then the pages would become huge and overcrowded with information. We also discarded this possibility.

We decided to use something in between these two extremes: We create one page describing how to perform a process step. As the wizard offers an expert and a novice mode, this page can be displayed to novice users and it can be hidden for experts, who do not need this information. In addition the atomic operations are spread over several pages. By default five atomic operations are grouped on one page. (According to Miller the short term memory has a capacity of 7 +/- 2 information items [9]. With five operations on one page one can be sure, that users are able to get all information displayed on the page.) But someone, who knows, how the user interfaces of the automated atomic operations look like, can group the operations in such a way that the automated operations fit well on the page. Therefore the "Additional Options" mode of WGT exists. This mode allows to group the atomic operations on the pages in a way that best fits the needs.

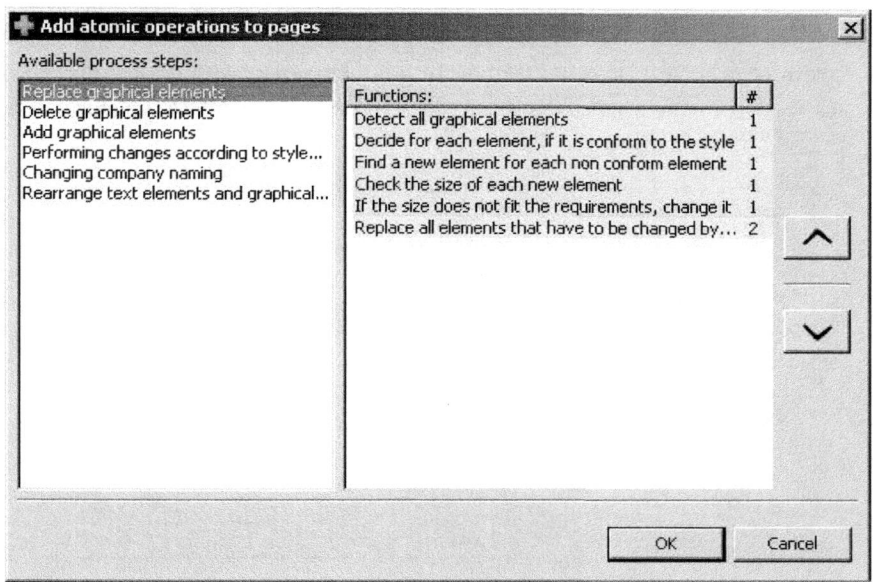

Fig. 6. Arranging atomic operations on pages

Figure 6 shows how a user can group atomic operations to pages. You can see that for each process step it is shown, which operations are needed in this step. On the right site it is possible to see which operations are placed on which page. By selecting an operation and pressing the arrows on the right you can move this operation to a page before or behind the actual page. Selecting for example the operation "If the size does not fit the requirements, change it" and pressing the "Down"-Arrow on the right would move this operation to the second page.

7   Step 3: Extension of Prototypic Wizard

Together with the process descriptions generated during the first step the wizard serves as a basis for communication between process experts and developers. Based on this prototype a common understanding of the process described in the wizard can be established. The wizard makes it easier to discuss ideas for further development in a vivid way. In addition it provides a code skeleton that can be enhanced comfortably by a developer. For this purpose the code generated by WGT is marked with special comments indicating, where additional code can be added. This can be done in the third step of the proceeding presented in this paper. The two steps presented so far are both executed by process experts. Step 3 has to be executed by a developer.

To make work faster and less error prone it is useful to add automated functionalities to the wizard, where this is reasonably possible. Therefore the wizard created by a process expert has to be handed over to a developer. The developer gets the information created in the first step and the prototype generated in the second step.

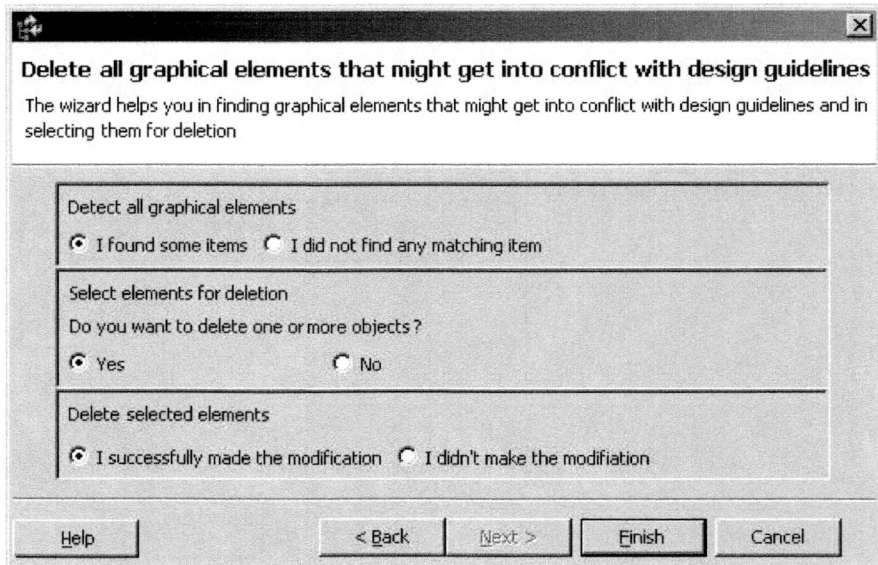

Fig. 7. One wizard page before adding automated functionalities

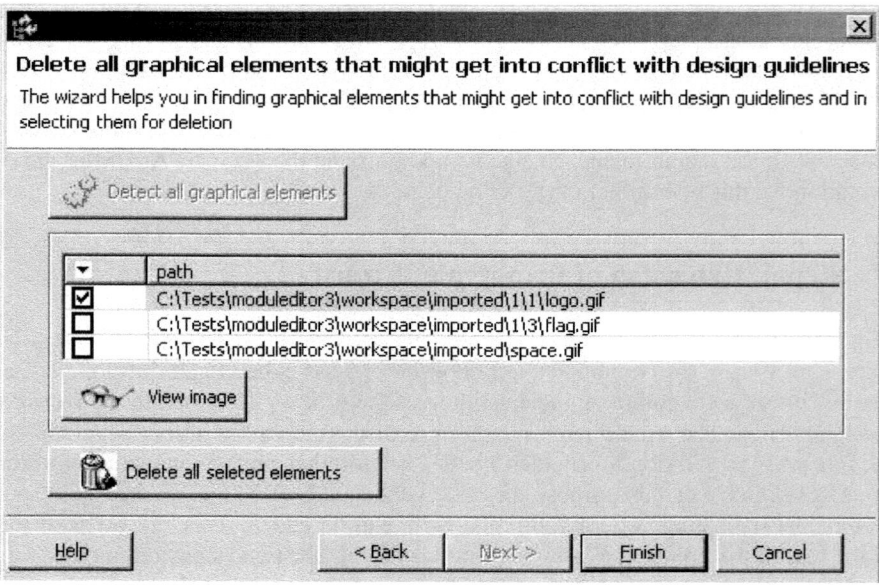

Fig. 8. The same page after adding automated functionalities

With the Wizard Generation Tool WGT for each process step one or more wizard pages have been created. The pages contain a list of all operations needed to execute the process steps. The developer can add additional source code for each operation that can be automated. The initial source code contains comments indicating, where automation is possible. The developer has to provide a new part of source code describing the user interface and a code section in the controller class (compare section 6) that stores the information needed for and provided by the operation. The operations itself are stored in a so called function pool. This allows to reuse operations in several process steps. Comments within the original source code give hints, where to enter the new code and which dependencies between model, view, and controller have to be taken into account.

By this proceeding it is possible to add code for all operations that can be automated. Figure 7 and figure 8 show a part of one wizard before and after adding automation to the operations. Together with the process expert the developer can check for each operation if it works in the desired way. By this proceeding we enhanced the prototype created based on the adaptations patterns to a fully functioning support tool for adaptation processes.

8 Application of the Approach to the Example Scenario

With the approach presented here we created a wizard supporting users in performing the adaptation processes described in chapter 2: We have written down the outcome of our user survey (compare section 2) using patterns to describe the adaptation processes. This led to a couple of initial patterns. We revised the initial patterns together with process experts. In addition we made sure to find at least three known uses for each pattern by searching for successful applications of the patterns. Some of the results have been published at PLoP conferences [20, 21]. Then we generated a prototypic wizard with WGT and enhanced the prototype by automated functions.

The resulting adaptation wizard is integrated into a larger tool, the so called repurposing suite, which is described in [8]. This suite allows to analyse, modularize, adapt, and aggregate existing E-Learning material. By embedding the adaptation tool into the repurposing suite user, we offer users a possibility to efficiently reuse existing E-learning material. Figure 9 shows the start screen of the tool, displaying all available adaptations.

The wizard is based on patterns describing the following adaptations:

- Adaptation to a changed (corporate) design: This adaptation is needed whenever the appearance of the material has to be changed, e.g. if material designed for one company has to be reused in another company with a different corporate design.
- Adaptation in order to achieve a print version: Often a separate print version is needed, that has to fit a certain paper size.
- Adaptation to a changed terminology: Sometimes the terminology changes, e.g. if the course is reused in another company that uses a different terminology.
- Adaptation to a changed language (i.e. translation), e.g. translate from English to German.
- Adaptation to achieve an accessible version, e.g. in order to achieve a version that is suited for blind persons.

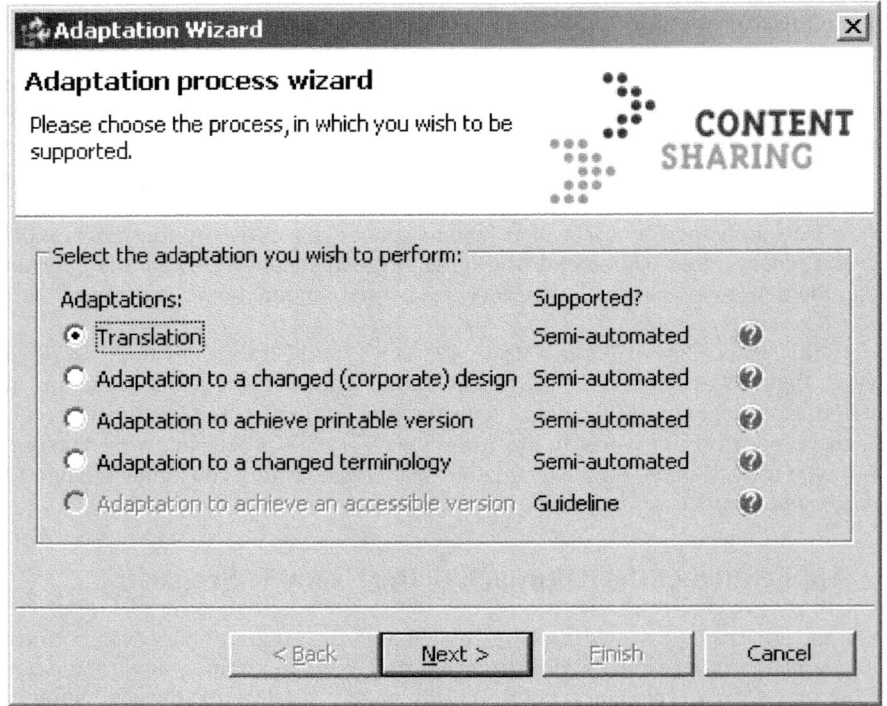

Fig. 9. Start page of the adaptation tool

For each adaptation one or more patterns exist describing the adaptation process. (The adaptation to achieve an accessible version is, for example, described by several patterns, as it consists of several sub-processes.) By entering the patterns into PIT and by adding all needed additional information about the processes, like process step descriptions and atomic operations descriptions, we created process descriptions. Then we generated a wizard with WGT based on these process descriptions. Outcome was a first prototype wizard (Figure 7 shows one page of this wizard).

The prototypic wizard guides users step by step through the adaptation processes. For each process a high level description is offered. This description provides general information what has to be taken into account, when performing the adaptation process. It is based on the patterns describing how this process helps to solve a specific problem. In addition detailed information about the process steps and atomic operation is offered. (This information has been created in addition to the patterns.)

As a next step we automated all parts of the wizard, where this was reasonably possible. (Figure 8 shows one of the pages enriched with automated functionalities.) We analysed the functions needed to perform the supported adaptation processes and we designed functionalities that could be used to enhance the prototype. These functionalities have been added to the wizard. Outcome of this proceeding was a tool that supports users in performing adaptation processes for E-Learning material.

If a user starts the adaptation tool (compare figure 9) she can see the degree of automation offered by the tool for each supported process. (At the moment four adaptation processes are partially automated. For all adaptation processes a detailed guideline is available, which can be accessed by clicking on the question mark on the right of the corresponding process.)

The adaptation tool offers support for novices and laymen, but it also is a valuable support for adaptation process experts in their daily work, as it automates several steps that by now often have to be done manually (e.g. when creating a print version). Thus the adaptation tool offers two modes: one for novices and one for experts. The mode for novices offers more detailed explanations whereas the mode for experts is optimized for working fast. (Of course experts also can get access to the detailed information, if they wish to.) A detailed explanation of the adaptation tool can be found in [18].

8.1 Evaluation of the Adaptation Tool

A first evaluation with test users of the Content Sharing Project was promising: The users were enabled to perform all offered adaptations correctly. They found process guidance and detailed help on all processes. Based on their feedback we improved the functionalities. In a second, larger evaluation we tested our tool by comparing it to a common WYSIWYG HTML editor. At the moment no tool exists that supports all adaptation processes that are needed to adapt existing E-Learning material to changed usage scenarios. Therefore we have chosen a tool that is comfortable to use and supports at least most of the functions needed to perform the adaptation processes to compare it with our tool. As many E-Learning courses are stored in HTML format we have chosen an HTML editor. We wanted a tool that is easy to use and that offers a WYSIWYG function allowing to control directly what has been changed. We decided to use Netscape Composer as HTML editor, as it is easy to use and allows to perform at least some typical adaptations.

We asked 32 users to perform some typical adaptations to three existing E-Learning courses. (It was possible to perform all adaptations with our tool as well as with Netscape Composer.) One E-Learning course was dealing with medical topics, one was an introduction to Multimedia, and the third one was a course to learn English. Half of the users were asked to work with our tool; the others got the WYSIWYG tool. Both groups got a detailed explanation how to use their tool. The tasks were the same for both groups. At the end of the test the participants were asked to answer a questionnaire in order to determine how satisfied they were in working with the tool.

Both groups were able to perform the adaptations as described in the manuals. Both groups did the tasks fast and with only very few errors. But we found that users working with our adaptation support tool needed in average 14 minutes with our tool to finish the tasks compared to in average 20 minutes with Netscape Composer. And users working with the Netscape Composer made in average twice as many mistakes as users working with the adaptation tool.) In addition users that were working with our tool were more satisfied with the use of the tool. As the adaptation tool got very positive feedback and the outcome of the adaptations had a very good quality, we think that our tool offers a better support for adaptation processes then the tool used for comparison. In addition we think that the knowledge collected with patterns is a good support for users in performing adaptations as the explanations how to use the tools for both test groups were based on the patterns. And the results for both test groups were very satisfying. For the future we plan to enhance our adaptation tool based on the feedback we got from the users.

All users, that have been taking part in the evaluation, have knowledge of the HTML file format. But one additional benefit of our tool is that this knowledge is not needed, as the tool abstracts from a concrete file format. Thus it is possible to use one tool to perform all adaptations in all files belonging to a learning resource without having detailed knowledge of the formats. This is a feature that is not supported by the tools that up to now have been used to perform adaptation processes.

9   Evaluation of Concept

The aim of the concept presented in this paper was, to enable adaptation process experts without knowledge of process modelling to describe adaptation processes by an easy to understand process description formalism and to create prototypic wizards that reflect the processes as they are performed by the process experts.

To evaluate if process experts are able to use the pattern based process description formalism and the wizard generation tool independent from their knowledge of common programming and modelling formalisms, we performed a user test with 32 users. Half of the persons had knowledge of process modelling and of IT related issues like programming. Half of the users did not have this kind of knowledge.

All persons were asked to describe the same process with the help of PIT and to generate a prototypic wizard based on their process descriptions by using WGT. It turned out that all users made very good process descriptions with only very few errors. Users without modelling and IT knowledge made some more errors then users with this kind of knowledge. (In average the difference was one error.) All users were able to generate a prototype that guides through the described process. Regarding the ability to generate the wizard there was no difference between the two user groups.

In addition all users gave a very positive feedback regarding the understandability and the manageability of both tools. Thus we assume that all users were able to use the pattern based process description formalism and the wizard generation tool in the intended way. We also got some feedback how to increase the usefulness of the tools and the resulting wizard. We plan to analyse this feedback and to take it as a basis for further improvements.

10   Unresolved Issues and Future Work

There are several unresolved issues concerning PIT and WGT. For the future we plan to work on these issues. In this section we give an overview on the unresolved issues.

PIT allows entering relationships between processes. These are taken into account when generating the wizard: If one process has been finished in the wizard, a hint to related processes is given. PIT also allows specifying forces and consequences. But at the moment these are not taken into account in the generated wizard. But we are thinking of how to realize this. One possibility would be to use the forces as well as the consequences to find out if a process is useful in a specific situation:

If users are not sure which process they have to perform, they can search the problem statements. This helps to limit the number of possible processes. In addition users should be able to browse through the consequences and forces. This also reduces the number of possible processes. If a process has been performed the consequences can again be shown to users to allow them, to decide if a second process is necessary to eliminate negative consequences.

At the moment the wizard generation tool WGT is a first prototype. The layout of the wizard has to be overdone by taking into account common HCI guidelines. Nevertheless the wizard as it is by now already offers a good starting point for further development and a valuable basis for communication between process experts and software developers, as the evaluation of the adaptation tool, which is based on such a wizard, has shown.

Additionally to serving a basis for communication, the prototype wizard also can be used as a starting point for further development. Therefore WGT adds comments to the automatically generated source code of the prototype. Those comments offer hints to a developer, where it is possible to change the source code of the prototype in order to add additional functionalities. But it might occur that a process expert decides to change the process description after a while and to create a new prototype wizard based on the changed description. The new wizard then does not contain the enhancements added by the developer before. At the moment this means that the developer again has to add the additional functionalities. For the future it is planned to develop a concept that allows to merge both versions.

We created the approach presented in this paper to support adaptation processes. But we believe that it also can be used for other kinds of processes. Thus we tested for several other kinds of processes, if it is possible to describe them with PIT.

We found that PIT also can be used to enter already existing patterns (that might have to be adapted to the pattern notation used here) as well as new patterns. We have successfully tested this with some of the security patterns presented in [16]. In addition we created new descriptions for the process of hiring new employees and for the process of booking journeys. For all these kinds of processes it turned out that it was possible to describe them with PIT and to create prototype wizards with WGT.

But it seems that there are other processes that cannot be described with PIT, e.g. processes with a focus on data flow. Thus, for the future it would be desirable to analyse which kinds of processes can be described with PIT and for which kinds of processes the approach presented here does not work.

When we were creating the E-Learning material adaptation wizard (compare section 8), we entered patterns as descriptions for the process and additional descriptions (not patterns) for the needed process steps and atomic operations. But as PIT only reassures that all needed information to perform a certain process is provided in the predefined structure, it has to be taken into account that the process descriptions provided by process experts might not meet common pattern criteria like being generic or having at least three known uses. It might occur that the process experts only create process descriptions that are written down in a pattern based notation formalism. But these descriptions also contain valuable knowledge and offer a good basis for the wizard creation. As the process expert is enabled to generate the wizard he or she can change the process description as many times as needed to achieve a wizard that really meets the experiences of the process experts.

Acknowledgments

The authors thank all persons, who supported this work by offering fruitful discussion or by encouraging us to proceed with our work. This paper is based on a paper presented at EuroPLoP 2008 [22]. Therefore we especially thank Michael Weiss, who provided a huge amount of helpful comments during shepherding for EuroPLoP 2008. Although many thanks go to our writer's workshop group at EuroPLoP 2008 for a very good discussion and so many useful hints.

The authors also thank SAP AG - SAP Research CEC Darmstadt, as well as KOM Multimedia Communications Lab at the Technical University of Darmstadt for supporting this work.

Part of this work is supported by the German Federal Ministry of Economics and Technology in the context of the project Content Sharing. This project was funded under the promotional reference "01 MD 404". The authors take the responsibility for the contents.

References

1. Business Process Modeling Notation Specification. Final Adopted Specification (2006), http://www.omg.org/docs/dtc/06-02-01.pdf
2. DIN En ISO 9241: Ergonomics of Human System Interaction. Part 11: Guidance on usability and part 110: Dialogue principles
3. Dreyfus, S.E., Dreyfus, H.L.: A five–stage model of the mental activities involved in directed skill acquisition. Unpublished report supported by the Air Force Office of Scientific Research (AFSC), USAF (Contract F49620–79–C–0063), University of Califonia at Berkley (1980)
4. Eckstein, R.: Java SE Application Design With MVC (2007), http://java.sun.com/developer/technicalArticles/javase/mvc/index.html
5. Folmer, E., van Welie, M., Bosch, J.: Bridging patterns: An approach to bridge gaps between SE and HCI. Information and Software Technology 48(2) (2006)
6. Fowler, M.: Analysis Patterns: Reusable Object Models. Addison-Wesley, Reading (1996)
7. Hahsler, M.: Analyse Patterns im Softwareentwicklungsprozeß. PhD thesis at WU Wien (2001)
8. Meyer, M., Hildebrandt, T., Rensing, C., Steinmetz, R.: Requirements and an Architecture for a Multimedia Content Re-purposing Framework. In: Nejdl, W., Tochtermann, K. (eds.) EC-TEL 2006. LNCS, vol. 4227, pp. 500–505. Springer, Heidelberg (2006)
9. Miller, G.A.: The Magical Number Seven, Plus or Minus Two: Some Limits on Our Capacity for Processing Information. The Psychological Review 63(2), 81–97 (1956)
10. Müller, S.: Modellbasierte IT-Unterstützung von wissensintensiven Prozessen - Dargestellt am Beispiel medizinischer Forschungsprozesse. PhD thesis at the Universität Erlangen - Nürnberg (2007)
11. PLML, XML DTD available under, http://www.hcipatterns.org/PLML+1.0.html
12. Robertson, S.: Requirements trawling: techniques for discovering requirements. International Journal of Human-Computer Studies 55(4) (October 2001)

13. Royce, W.W.: Managing the Development of Large Software Systems. In: Proceedings of the 9th International Conference on Software Engineering (1987)
14. Scheer, A.-W.: CIOs entwickeln sich zu Chief Process Officers. In: CIO (2007), http://www.cio.de/karriere/cios_im_portrait/810380/index4.html
15. Shneiderman, B., Plaisant, C.: Designing the user interface. Addison Wesley, Reading (2004)
16. Schumacher, M., Fernandez, E., Hybertson, D., Buschmann, F., Sommerlad, P.: Security Patterns - Integrating Security and Systems Engineering. John Wiley & Sons, Chichester (2005)
17. Siau, K., Ericksson, J., Lee, L.: Theoretical versus practical complexity: The case of UML. Journal of Database Management 16(3) (2005)
18. Zimmermann, B.: Pattern-basierte Prozessbeschreibung und –unterstützung. Ein Werkzeug zur Unterstützung von Prozessen zur Anpassung von E-Learning-Materialien. PhD thesis at the Technische Universität Darmstadt, Germany (2008)
19. Zimmermann, B., Bergsträßer, S., Rensing, C., Steinmetz, R.: A Requirements Analysis of Adaptations of Re-Usable (E-Learning) Content. In: Proceedings of World Conference on Educational Multimedia, Hypermedia and Telecommunications (2006)
20. Zimmermann, B., Rensing, C., Steinmetz, R.: Patterns for Tailoring E-Learning Materials to Make them Suited for Changed Requirement. Published in the Proceedings of Viking-PLoP 2006 (2006)
21. Zimmermann, B., Rensing, C., Steinmetz, R.: Patterns towards Making Web Material Accessible. Published in the Proceedings of EuroPLoP 2007 (2007)
22. Zimmermann, B., Rensing, C., Steinmetz, R.: Experiences in Using Patterns to Support Process Experts in Wizard Creation. Published in the Proceedings of EuroPLoP 2008 (2008)

Appendix

Patterns Mentioned in This Paper

This paper mentions several patterns that already have been published. Here a short overview of those patterns is listed in order to get an idea what the patterns are about. The patterns can be found in [20, 21].

- *Design adaptation*: This adaptation occurs for example if material created for one company is reused in another company. Then often the layout of the material has to be changed in order to fit to the corporate design of the new company. The pattern helps to adapt the design.
- *Printability*: Often web content is optimized for working with it on a computer screen. But many readers want to print out at least parts of the material. Then a print optimized version has to be created. The solution of the pattern describes how a separate print version can be created.
- *Translation*: If a part of the target group does not understand the language in which the material is provided, the material has to be translated to one or more other languages. This pattern describes how to perform a translation and what has to be taken into account before, during, and after translating the text.
- *Correct Arrangement of Elements*: There are several adaptations where it is needed to change the arrangement of the elements of your material in order to make the arrangement suited for the new requirements. This pattern describes how you can re-arrange the elements in a way that they comply with the requirements.
- *Correct Length of Text Blocks*: If you have to exchange text parts with other text parts it often occurs that the length of the new part is different than the one of the original text part. Then you have to change the size in a way that it fits to the requirements. This pattern presents two possibilities how you can correct the length of a text block: You can shorten or lengthen its content.
- *Attached Transcriptions*: When creating an additional version suited for blind persons it might occur that an attached text transcript for pure audio information has to be provided.
- *Sign Language Videos*: When creating an additional version suited for blind persons it might occur that videos enhanced by sign language to "translate" the audio information of the video have to be provided.

Input Form of PIT

The process description input tool PIT supports adaptation process experts in creating process description of adaptation processes. It has been described in section 6. Figure 10 shows the main input form of PIT.

Name *

Please enter the name of the process you are describing. ⊘

Adaptation of (corporate) design

Intent

What is the main purpose of the process? ⊘

Adapt the design of materials to match incoming requirements.

Context

In which context does the process help? ⊘

As for many kinds of content the design is very important for E-Learning content. Therefore you should always take care of a design matching all requirements. If there is a change in design requirements it is necessary to adapt the course to the new requirements. There are several reasons for a change in the requirements, e.g. if a course was originally designed for one company and should be re-used in another company or if the style guide of a company changes.

Problem *

Which problem is solved by the process? ⊘

You want to adapt your course to changed requirements concerning the (corporate) design. What do you have to do in order to achieve a design that fits the new requirements?

Example

Please enter an example where the process can be applied.   ⊘

Image for example: design.png   📁 Browse

Explanation for example:

The example shows a course: First the original version, and then after adapting it to a changed corporate design.

Forces *

Which external forces have an influence on the process?   ⊘

enter >   An influence   ➕ Add

⊗   E-Learning courses are normally designed by following a style guide. If this style guid...
      The design normally consists of many items, like logos, background images and colors...
⌃   If a style template is used you can change this template (e.g. CSS for HTML or slide ...
      If no style template is used you have to change the design by changing element by ...   ⚙ Edit
⌄

⊗   ✕ Delete

Solution *

Please describe how to perform the process.   ⊘

A design adaptation starts by replacing graphical elements that do not meet the
requirements (e.g. logos). Therefore you decide for each graphical element if it is conform to
your requirements. If it is not you replace it by a conform element. If the new graphical elements
have a different size compared to the original ones it might be necessary to resize them.
Depending on the file format of the materials the way how you replace the elements is different.
E.g. in HTML you replace the target of the element's tag, whereas in DOC you delete the old

Steps needed to perform the solution: *

Caution: The steps are performed in the order given below!   ⊘

	Name	Execution	type	
⊗	Replacing graphical elements	is optional		➕ Add
⌃	Deleting graphical elements	is optional		
	Add additional graphical elements	is optional		⚙ Edit
	Performing changes according to style gu...	is optional		
⌄	Changing company naming	is optional		

Fig. 10. Part of PIT's input form

XML Files Generated by PIT

PIT stores the process description given by the process experts in XML format (compare section 5). The following listing shows the DTD of the XML files containing the process information.

```
<!ELEMENT pattern (intent?, context?, problem,
example_illustration?, example_explanation?, forces,
solution, process_steps, known_uses*, consequences,
related-patterns>
<!ATTLIST pattern patternID ID #REQUIRED
confidence CDATA #IMPLIED
name CDATA #REQUIRED >
<!ELEMENT intent (#PCDATA)>
<!ELEMENT context (#PCDATA)>
<!ELEMENT problem (#PCDATA)>
<!ELEMENT example_illustration (#PCDATA)>
<!ELEMENT example_explanation (#PCDATA)>
<!ELEMENT forces (force*)>
<!ELEMENT force EMPTY>
<!ATTLIST force name CDATA #REQUIRED>
<!ELEMENT solution (#PCDATA)>
<!ELEMENT Process_steps (Process_step+)>
<!ELEMENT Process_step EMPTY>
<!ATTLIST Process_step
name Name #REQUIRED
mandatory (true | false) "true">
<!ELEMENT known_uses (#PCDATA)>
<!ELEMENT consequences
(positive_consequence+, negative_consequence*)>
<!ELEMENT positive_consequence EMPTY>
<!ATTLIST positive_consequence name CDATA #REQUIRED>
<!ELEMENT negative_consequence EMPTY>
<!ATTLIST negative_consequence name CDATA #REQUIRED>
<!ELEMENT related_patterns (related_pattern*)>
<!ELEMENT Related_patterns (Related_pattern*)>
<!ELEMENT Related_pattern EMPTY>
<!ATTLIST Related_pattern
name CDATA #REQUIRED
patternID ID #REQUIRED
            type CDATA #REQUIRED
>
```

Listing 1. Pattern file DTD

The information about the process flow is stored as a process graph. The following listing shows a part of such a process graph stored in XML (compare section 6.1). You can see a process identified via its ID. All process steps needed to perform the process are listed in the "requires" section of the process. For each process step it is noted if the step has to be performed (mandatory="true") or not (mandatory="false").

The last process step in the example is only performed if at least one of the steps before has been performed. Therefore all process steps, which can be performed before this step, are listed in the "precondition" section of the last process step. For the first process step you can see all atomic operations needed to perform this step. Again it is written down for each operation if the execution is mandatory. In addition you can see the three kinds of atomic operations (query, decision, and execution). The original file also contains a section defining the needed atomic operations. This section is not shown in the listing below.

```
<process id="process_pattern$56667" process-
pattern="true">
  <requires fragmentRef="process_step$22357234"
  mandatory="false"/>
  <requires fragmentRef="process_step$25517184"
  mandatory="false"/>
  <requires fragmentRef="process_step$28757034"
  mandatory="false"/>
  <requires fragmentRef="process_step$36740146"
  mandatory="false"/>
  <requires fragmentRef="process_step$43532108"
  mandatory="false"/>
  <requires fragmentRef="process_step$50025522"
  mandatory="true">
    <precondition fragmentRef="process_step$22357234"/>
    <precondition fragmentRef="process_step$25517184"/>
    <precondition fragmentRef="process_step$28757034"/>
    <precondition fragmentRef="process_step$36740146"/>
    <precondition fragmentRef="process_step$43532108"/>
  </requires>
</process>
<process-step id="process_step$22357234">
  <requires functionRef="query$28693719"
  mandatory="true"/>
  <requires functionRef="decision$26294026"
  mandatory="true"/>
  <requires functionRef="decision$24376617"
  mandatory="false"/>
  <requires functionRef="query$23537464"
  mandatory="false"/>
  <requires functionRef="decision$32687500"
  mandatory="false"/>
  <requires functionRef="query$33442589"
  mandatory="false"/>
  <requires functionRef="execution$5472454"
  mandatory="false"/>
  <requires functionRef=" execution $51555041"
  mandatory="false"/>
</process-fragment>
```

Listing 2. Part of a process graph file

Modifiers: Increasing Richness and Nuance of Design Pattern Languages

Gwendolyn L. Kolfschoten[1], Robert O. Briggs[2], and Stephan Lukosch[1]

[1] Department of Systems Engineering, Faculty of Technology, Policy, and Management,
Delft University of Technology
{G.L.Kolfschoten,S.G.Lukosch}@tudelft.nl
[2] Center for Collaboration Science, College of Business Administration,
University of Nebraska at Omaha
rbriggs@unomaha.edu

Abstract. One of the challenges when establishing and maintaining a pattern language is to balance richness with simplicity. On the one hand, designers need a variety of useful design patterns to increase the speed of their design efforts and to reduce design risk. On the other hand, the greater the variety of design patterns in a language, the higher the cognitive load to remember and select among them. One solution to this problem is the concept of a modifier design pattern, a design pattern for pattern languages. A modifier pattern is a named, documented variation that can be applied to some set of other design patterns. They create similar, useful changes and refinements to the solutions derived from any pattern to which they are applied. The modifier concept, described in this paper emerged in a relatively new design pattern language for collaborative work practices in which the design patterns are called thinkLets. When analyzing the thinkLet pattern language, we found that many of the patterns we knew were variations and refinements of other patterns. However, we also found patterns in these variations; we found variations that could be applied to different patterns, with similar effects. We document these variations as modifiers. In this paper, we introduce the concept of modifier design patterns and illustrate the use of modifiers with two case studies.

1 Introduction

Design patterns were first described by Alexander [1] as re-usable solutions to address frequently occurring problems. In Alexander's words: "a [design] pattern describes a problem which occurs over and over again and then describes the core of the solution to that problem, in such a way that you can use this solution a million times over, without ever doing it the same way twice"[1 p x]. After the "gang of four" created a collection of patterns for software engineering [2], the concept entered a variety of domains including collaboration support. For example, Lukosch and Schümmer [3] propose a pattern language for the development of collaborative software. Design patterns are successfully used in related fields such as communication software [4], e-learning [5] and for knowledge management [6]. Design patterns have various functions. They provide designers with building blocks for their design

J. Noble et al. (Eds.): TPLOP II, LNCS 6510, pp. 62–78, 2011.

efforts, they can be used to capture best practices, they support teaching and training, and they become a shared language among the users of the design patterns. Pattern languages are often authored by one or more authors, however, ideally, a pattern language becomes a living document, used and maintained by a community of designers, who update their patterns when new experiences give rise to new patterns.

One of the challenges when establishing and maintaining a pattern language is to balance richness with simplicity. On the one hand, designers need a variety of useful design patterns to increase the speed of their design efforts and to reduce design risk, basing their design on best practices. A pattern language with a greater number of design patterns offers a larger variety for inspiration and choice. With more relevant options, there are more circumstances where it is possible to establish a good fit between the design problem and design-pattern-based solution. On the other hand, the greater the variety of design patterns in a language, the higher the cognitive load to remember and select among them. A community of practice for a pattern language must therefore strive for parsimony. The community must attempt to capture useful and important design patterns, while keeping the design patterns consistent, coherent, interlinked and perhaps most importantly, non-overlapping. The need for parsimony conflicts with the need for greater variety and utility.

The modifier concept (described below in a design pattern) provides a useful device for maintaining the parsimony of a pattern language while adding richness and nuance to its range of possibilities. A *modifier* is a specific type of design pattern. It is a named, documented variation that can be applied to a collection of design patterns with a similar effect. Modifiers create similar, useful changes or refinements in the solution derived from any pattern to which the modifier is applied.

The modifier concept emerged in a relatively new design pattern language called, thinkLets [7, 8]. *ThinkLets* is a pattern language for designing collaborative work practices. In this paper, we present a formal articulation of the modifier concept, written as a design pattern for pattern languages. We first explain the origins and nature of the modifier concept and argue its utility as an extension to a pattern language. Next, we will show in two case studies how the modifier concept can be used to simplify a pattern language and articulate the special status of modifiers as reusable variations to other patterns. Finally, we discuss the need for and value of the modifier concept in pattern languages in general.

2   The Modifier Design Pattern

Context: The pattern language you (or your community) are developing is steadily growing to a point where it creates cognitive overload for its users. It seems an infinite number of patterns could be added to the language.

Problem: When patterns in your pattern language are compared, they are found to be quite similar, yet there are important differences that need to be captured in the pattern language to transfer important nuances to solutions. These nuances increase the complexity of the pattern language and thereby users of the pattern language suffer from cognitive overload. Design pattern documentation often has a section that identifies related patterns and useful combinations of patterns. Addressing these nuances in the related patterns section of the pattern does not help, as using a related pattern is different than using patterns in combinations and a pattern can be a supplement to another pattern (addition), a variation, an alternative, or a refinement. All these distinctions are difficult to articulate.

Symptoms: You should consider applying this pattern, when ...
- The pattern language you are authoring seems to explode in size.
- New patterns are continuously found but many patterns are similar.
- Some of the similar patterns might be defined on different abstraction levels.
- Some of the similar patterns seem to have a unique aspect that conveys a deliberately and usefully different design choice.
- It is difficult to merge similar patterns into a single pattern as this requires the explanation of many design choices in one pattern.
- The same variation or refinement of design choice appears in many patterns.

Solution: Use modifiers to reduce the complexity of a pattern language and the cognitive overload for the users of the pattern language. Modifiers are named, documented, reusable variations or refinements that can be applied to a set of design patterns in order to create a similar effect to the solutions derived from these patterns. The modifier is a specific type of design pattern. Modifiers are design patterns that are used in combination with other design patterns, either as a variation, a small change in the design pattern, or as a refinement, a nuance in the design pattern. Modifiers alone typically do not present a complete design solution; they become only valuable when combined with other design patterns.

Metaphor: The modifier concept can be compared to aspect-oriented programming. As in aspect-oriented programming, a recurring variation is captured separately to improve overview and clarity of the whole. In one sense, a modifier is to a design pattern as a virus is to a cell. A virus is not a living organism, because on its own it cannot respire, digest, or reproduce. A virus, however, invokes predictable changes in the way the cell performs. A given virus may create similar effects on many different kinds of cells, but there are some kinds of cells that a given virus cannot affect. In like manner, modifiers are a specific type of design pattern because on their own they cannot be used to invoke a robust, repeatable solution to a recurring problem. They can, however, invoke similar changes or refinements in the solutions derived from a collection of patterns.

Rationale: By using modifiers, you can add nuances to a set of more basic design patterns without suffering a combinatorial explosion of the pattern language. When modifiers are distilled from a set of design patterns, the pattern language can become richer, as more combinations can be made from fewer elements. At the same time, the pattern language becomes more concise as the number of concepts in the pattern language remains limited.

Pattern languages are used to transfer expert knowledge in a way that makes it easy to use. Design patterns are combined and/or interlinked in a pattern language. While relations with other patterns are often indicated, their nature is usually not discussed in detail. Some patterns can be used to offer several functionalities or methods that are jointly used to achieve a goal. Other patterns are variations or refinements; they are combined in a more integrated way to create a nuance to another pattern. When the same variations or refinements can be used in combination with several patterns, it becomes valuable to distinguish the role of this variation in the pattern language, to highlight its applicability to multiple patterns.

The modifier pattern helps to describe such combinations and refinements. In addition, the modifier can reduce the complexity of a pattern language by reducing its size. Patterns provide a vocabulary to be used in conversations [9]. Similarly, modifiers allow pattern authors to capture unique aspects that convey design choices which appear in many patterns but which on their own would not have been worth adding to the pattern language. By capturing such design choices in modifiers and thus abstracting them, modifiers offer guidance in applying sequences of design choices and reduce the complexity of design choices.

Danger spots: A difficulty in implementing modifiers in a pattern language is to distinguish recurring variations from truly different design patterns. A rule of thumb we used is that a modifier must be applicable to multiple patterns, and that a modifier by itself, may not provide a complete solution to a design created with the pattern language.

Examples:

- We found that the idea of variation exists in software design patterns as the 'refine' concept, defined by [10] "A specific pattern refines a more abstract pattern if the specific pattern's full description is a direct extension of the more general pattern. That is, the specific pattern must deal with a specialization of the problem the general pattern addresses, must have a similar (but more specialized) solution structure, and must address the same forces as the more general pattern, but may also address additional forces." This author, however, describes 'refine' in terms closer to object-oriented inheritance than to a variation that can be applied across many patterns. Nonetheless, when multiple refine relations exist with a single design pattern, an opportunity may exist to simplify the pattern language through the use of modifiers.

- A second example can be found in the famous pattern language of Coplien and Harrison [11] on organizational design patterns. In this pattern language a key cornerstone is the pattern "community of trust," which explains that trust is the basis for successful teams and a requirement for various other patterns to work. However, on its own, trust does not prescribe how organizations should be designed the way other patterns in the language prescribe how roles and tasks and collaboration can be designed to successfully design the organization. Coplien and Harrison discuss why "community of trust" is a pattern. They explain it has structural impact on the organizational design and that there is a specific 'trick' to build trust described in "community of trust". The modifier concept will allow them to specifically position trust as a variation to many of the other patterns. In this way they can emphasize its critical nature, its effect in combination with other patterns, and the effect of the absence of trust in other patterns. In this case, however, the "community of trust" pattern is deemed a mandatory precondition to all other patterns in the pattern language. In the general case, modifiers would not necessarily be mandatory; the patterns they modify would be useful design solutions on their own, but their utility could be extended to a larger number of problems through the use of modifiers.

- A similar phenomenon can be found in the work of [12]. Their pattern language includes both design patterns and advice for the management of distributed development teams. Advice patterns are not intended to actually structure the work of team members, but rather they describe conditions required for the patterns to work. This is similar to the modifier concept and enables the pattern authors to keep their pattern language simple and yet rich with advice.
- The design of sites [13] clusters web sites into genres which offer customizable content and have their own audiences. For each of these genre patterns, the authors list a number of further patterns that can be applied to web sites of the identified genre. The HOMEPAGE PORTAL can be used for the genre patterns: PERSONAL E-COMMERCE, NONPROFITS AS NETWORKS OF HELP, VALUABLE COMPANY SITES, etc. Thus, the HOMEPAGE PORTAL servers as a modifier to various other patterns.

3   Case Study Evidence

To validate the need and use of the modifier design pattern we will discuss its use in two pattern languages. After describing these pattern languages we will show how modifiers were mined. We will give several examples of modifiers and their role in the pattern language, and finally, we will discuss the value of the modifiers to increase richness and to improve the structure in the pattern language, reducing its complexity.

3.1   Case 1: The Use of Modifiers in the thinkLet Pattern Language

Nature of the Pattern Language

ThinkLet design patterns were originally derived to document the techniques and best practices of expert facilitators. Facilitators are group-process professionals who design collaborative work practices and conduct the processes on behalf of groups. The thinkLets pattern language became more rigorously codified and refined with the advent of the newly emerging field of Collaboration Engineering. *Collaboration Engineering* is a specialty within the field of Facilitation. It is an approach to designing collaborative work practices for high value recurring tasks and deploying the designs to practitioners to execute for themselves without the ongoing intervention of facilitators [14]. ThinkLets, therefore, serve three different user groups; practitioners, who use thinkLets as scripts to support group work, facilitators, who use thinkLets to exchange best practices in facilitation, and collaboration engineers; who use thinkLets to rigorously design collaborative work practices and supporting technology in order to transfer these to practitioners. The thinkLet design patterns play a critical role in the transfer of the highly experience-based expertise of group process facilitation.

Mining Modifiers

Early in the life of the thinkLets pattern language, the utility of the concept gave rise to an explosion of design patterns. Designers quickly hit information overload, so researchers began work to see whether they could distill the burgeoning collection down to an essential set [15]. This research revealed that a number of the early thinkLets were useful variations on more fundamental design patterns, and many of these variations could be applied to a variety of design patterns. In total, the thinkLet pattern language contains more than 30 thinkLet design patterns and more than 10 modifiers.

Examples of Design Patterns and Modifiers in the Pattern Language

Table 1 summarizes five thinkLets. Note that these descriptions are not complete design pattern documentation, but rather a brief overview of the collaboration technique sufficient for the reader to understand the nature of the design pattern. For more information about the thinkLet set and the pattern language we refer to [7, 8, 16].

Table 1. Examples of thinkLets

thinkLet Example	Brief summary of the thinkLet
LEAFHOPPER	All participants view a set of pages, one page for each of several discussion topics. Each participant hops among the topics to add ideas as inspired by interest and expertise.
GOLDMINER	Participants view a page containing a collection of ideas, perhaps from an earlier brainstorming activity. They work in parallel, moving the ideas they deem most worthy of more attention from the original page to another page.
ILLUMINATOR	Participants review a page of contributions for clarity. When a participant judges a contribution to be vague or ambiguous, s/he requests clarification. Other group members offer explanations and the group agrees to a shared definition. If necessary, the group revises the contribution to better convey its agreed meaning.
POPCORNSORT	Participants work in parallel to move ideas from an unorganized list into labeled categories using a first-come-first-served protocol for deciding who gets to move each idea into a category.
STRAWPOLL	Moderator posts a page of unevaluated contributions. Participants are instructed to rate each item on a designated scale using designated criteria. Participants are told that they are not making a decision, just getting a sense of the group's opinions to help focus subsequent discussion.

We will now describe three modifiers in Table 2. Modifiers are not complete design patterns, but rather named, codified variations that can be applied to one or more thinkLets to create similar changes in the function of the thinkLet. Modifier documentation includes the name, purpose, and rule-change for the modifier, and a short explanation of effects the modifier will create. In thinkLet documentation, we identify the modifiers that can be applied to the thinkLet. In modifier documentation, we identify the thinkLets to which a modifier can be applied.

Table 2. Examples of thinkLet modifiers

Modifier	Brief summary of the modifier
ONE UP	Participants are instructed that each new contribution must be better than existing contributions according some specified criteria. For example, "Please give me an idea that is more flexible than those we already have. Please suggest an idea that would be cheaper…" This encourages the contribution of ideas with specific desired qualities [17].
IDENTIFICATION	Let participants choose to identify who executed certain actions; e.g. add, edit, evaluate, delete. Some thinkLets, by default, let groups act anonymously. In many cases, this has a positive effect on willingness to contribute. Other times, however, it is useful to allow identification, which enables participants to receive credit for or be held accountable for their actions, or to emphasize their expertise, their stake, or their_role. [18].
CHAUFFEURED	Instead of working in parallel, where each participant takes separate individual actions, participants jointly decide what action should be taken; e.g. joint organizing, joint clarification/rephrasing, joint evaluation. One participant serves as chauffeur for the group, actually taking the action in accordance with the wishes of the group. While parallel work can be more efficient than chauffeured work, in some cases it is more valuable to ensure shared understanding and reach mutually acceptable agreements than it is to be more efficient

Table 3 shows that each modifier can be applied to several thinkLets. For instance, OneUp can be used as a variation to LEAFHOPPER to stimulate excellence of contributions on a specific criterion, but can be used for ILLUMINATOR in the same manner to stimulate contributions are exceeding others on a specific criterion. IDENTIFICATION can be used in combination with various thinkLets to encourage or enable participants to take ownership, and chauffeuring can be used across thinkLets to create buy-in and ownership of choices. With the modifier concept, a user who learned eight patterns - five thinkLets and three modifiers – can wield them to create 14 solutions. Without the modifier concept the pattern language would require fourteen patterns to capture the same solutions. Thus, the modifier concept can make a pattern language both richer and more parsimonious.

Table 3. Implications of modifiers on different patterns of collaboration, and the thinkLets within it

<table>
<tr><th colspan="5" align="center">Modifiers</th></tr>
<tr><td></td><td></td><td>One up</td><td>Identification</td><td>Chauffeured</td></tr>
<tr><td rowspan="5">thinkLets</td><td>LeafHopper</td><td>Generate contributions that excel on specified criteria</td><td>Authorship of contributions / Editorship for changed contributions</td><td>People suggest contributions, a recorder writes them down</td></tr>
<tr><td>GoldMiner</td><td>Select /summarize to converge on contributions that excel on specified criteria</td><td>Authorship of abstractions, summaries; identity of those who select or reject a contribution</td><td>Participants discuss which ideas are worthy of more attention, a chauffeur documents the choices</td></tr>
<tr><td>Illuminator</td><td>Clarify how a new contribution exceeds others with respect to specified criteria</td><td>Lobbying, explanation from specific author's perspective</td><td>Participants discuss shared meaning, a recorder documents their decisions</td></tr>
<tr><td>PopcornSort</td><td>Participants only move items to a category that they judge to be better in some way than those already appearing in a category</td><td>Identify those who create, change, or delete relationships among contributions</td><td>Participants discuss relationships among contributions, a chauffeur documents the relationships</td></tr>
<tr><td>StrawPoll</td><td></td><td>Display of polling results by pseudonym, by role, or by participant name.</td><td>Participants discuss the value of concepts toward goal attainment. A chauffeur records their evaluations.</td></tr>
</table>

Use of the Modifier Concept to Increase Richness and Nuance in the Pattern Language

We compared the underlying rules for seven idea-generation (brainstorming) thinkLets [19], LEAFHOPPER, and six other thinkLets, not described in this paper. The analysis revealed that there were superficial differences. Some of those thinkLets were, at the level of their essential rules, virtually identical. Thus, the seven thinkLets could be collapsed to an essential set of four. In that same set of seven thinkLets, however, we found 12 variations that could be abstracted, and then deliberately added to or removed from any thinkLet in the set to create a specific variation in its effect. These differences we captured as 12 named modifiers. The 12 modifiers we derived could be applied in various combinations to create variations on one or more of the four basic idea generation thinkLets [15, 19]. The four thinkLets and 12 modifiers that emerged could be combined in a total of 43 combinations. Without the modifier concept, the pattern language would have therefore required 43 thinkLets to capture those useful variations. With the modifier concept, the same design power can be obtained with only 16 concepts – the four thinkLets and 12 modifiers. Thus, by distilling the thinkLets and modifiers out of the 7 thinkLets, we uncovered 43 new design possibilities, and yet maintained the parsimony of the pattern language at 16 components.

3.2   Case 2: The Use of Modifiers in the Pattern Language for Computer Mediated Interaction

Nature of the Pattern Language

The pattern language for computer-mediated interaction (P4CMI) collects best practices from the last twenty years of research and development in the area of computer-supported collaborative work. This pattern language helps developers and end-users better understand computer-mediated interaction and design applications for effective computer-mediated interaction. The pattern language for computer-mediated interaction [20] evolved over the last five years and currently contains 71 patterns. P4CMI identifies 11 categories that group the 71 patterns according to the patterns' most important forces. In addition, P4CMI introduces abstraction levels to show which patterns will be used by whom in the development process. Patterns at a high abstraction level have their main focus on the social process (like the WELCOME AREA pattern that describes how to list new members of a group or community at a prominent place and introduce them to other members) while patterns on a low abstraction level have their main focus on the technical support (such as the CENTRALIZED OBJECTS pattern that describes how shared objects can be accessed from a common location). The idea of the language was born after we observed that the same concepts recurred in the CSCW research arena whenever a new base technology was available. After using the first patterns with end-users and software developers, it became clear that a special form of the patterns is required that can be understood both by end-users and software developers. The reason for this is that patterns for computer-mediated interaction always address a *socio-technical* problem: They have to describe the technology that supports the *group process* and therefore include a technical and a social aspect. Patterns for computer-mediated interaction are thus *socio-technical patterns*. Due to the socio-technical perspective on groupware design [21], the patterns for computer-mediated interaction try to predict the reciprocal effect of changes to either the social or the technical system and are embedded in a development process [22], which encourages the involved actors to frequent reflection on the system in order to best meet end-users requirements.

Mining Modifiers

The P4CMI pattern language is highly connected. The 71 patterns are grouped within 11 clusters that focus on different issues in the development of tools for computer-mediated interaction. On the top level, clusters deal with questions that arise around building a community while on the lower level, clusters deal with shared data management issues. Though these topics are at first glance not related, each pattern in P4CMI has a special-related patterns section that lists not only related patterns within P4CMI but also within another pattern language. On average, each pattern lists three to four related patterns. When considering the modifier pattern it became clear that some of the patterns in the P4CMI language are perfect candidates for modifiers, as they are cannot be used on their own but in combination with other patterns. In the following section, we report on modifiers which emerged from recurring pattern sequences within software development projects.

Table 4. Examples of P4CMI patterns

Pattern example	Brief summary of the pattern
USER GALLERY	You are building a system in which users should actively participate in a community. The users are identifiable by their real name or a nickname. To allow users to know who is using the system and to establish collaboration, you provide a list of all users who are members of the community.
HALL OF FAME	Your community system allows users to contribute their capabilities to the community. You now want to encourage active users to even greater efforts. For that purpose, you provide a list of those participants who contribute most and calculate the participants' contribution level with respect to the degree that they have helped others.
USER LIST	Many users are working synchronously on a set of shared artifacts, but users do not know with whom they are interacting or could interact. Consequently, they do not have a feeling of participating in a group. To provide awareness in context, you show who is currently accessing an artifact or participating in a collaborative session.
BUDDY LIST	You are using an interaction space such as a communication channel, a groupware application, or a collaborative virtual environment, together with many other users. When many users are able to interact in the interaction space, it is hard to maintain an overview of relevant interaction partners, since the number of users exceeds the number of relevant contacts for a specific user. For that purpose, you provide buddy lists where a user can bookmark other users who are of interest.
VIRTUAL ME	Users are interacting with each other in a collaborative system. In a large user community, account names look similar. To allow users to communicate their identity in interaction with other users, you provide them with means of creating a virtual identity that represents them while they act in the system and how the virtual identity when the user is active.

Examples of Design Patterns and Modifiers in the Pattern Language

Table 4 briefly summarizes the context, problem, and solution of several patterns from the P4CMI pattern language. Patterns in this set relate to possible or current partners for collaboration. The patterns mainly differ in the scope of the user community to be presented in the user interface. The complete patterns contain various additional sections to let the pattern serve as a socio-technical pattern which can be used as a language between end-users and developers during a software development project. For a complete description of each pattern, please refer to [20].

Table 5 describes three modifiers. In the P4CMI language, these modifiers are described as full design patterns. Each of the modifiers can be applied to a set of other patterns, yielding a similar effect that only differs in the scale of pattern to which the modifier is applied. In development projects, the combination of the modifiers in Table 5 with the patterns in Table 4 occurred quite often in structure-preserving transformations [23]. The recurrence of the pattern sequences in these transformations and the fact the patterns have so far not been used on their own strongly indicate that these patterns have to be used in combination with other patterns.

Table 5. Examples of P4CMI modifiers

Modifier	Brief summary of the modifier
AVAILABILITY STATUS	To allow spontaneous interaction, users have to be open to contact requests. However, each request disturbs the user or group contacted in their current task. To overcome this problem, you include an indicator in the application that signals the user's availability and how the user would react to an interaction.
ALIVENESS INDICATOR	Users who work mainly asynchronously only experience a small subset of activities that take place in the collaboration space. Specifically, they cannot easily see whether other users have been active during their absence. For that purpose, show an indicator with the user's virtual representation. For users that have performed activities in the collaboration space recently, use a picture for their indicator that looks very alive. Use gradually less lively pictures to represent periods of inactivity.
ACTIVITY INDICATOR	In a collocated setting, users are accustomed to perceive non-verbal signals such as movement or sounds when another user is active. If the users are distributed, these signals are missing. Therefore, indicate other user's current activities in the user interface. To reduce interruptions, use a peripheral place or a visually unobtrusive indicator.

Table 6 briefly describes the effect of applying the identified modifiers to the selected P4CMI patterns. The effect differs basically in the scale of the pattern. In the case of the USER GALLERY, all actors within a collaborative space are affected, whereas in the case of VIRTUAL ME, only the representation of a single actor is changed. Interestingly, all three modifiers can be applied to one pattern at once. In the case of a USER LIST, this would result in a USER LIST showing which group members are available, whether they are still active in the group, as well as what they are currently doing.

Table 6. Implications of modifiers on different P4CMI patterns

		Modifiers		
		AVAILABILITY STATUS	ALIVENESS INDICATOR	ACTIVITY INDICATOR
Patterns	USER GALLERY	Show which users are currently available.	Show which users are still active in the community.	Show the current activities of the available users.
	HALL OF FAME	Show which experts are currently available.	Show which experts are still active in the community.	Show the current activities of the experts.
	USER LIST	Show which group members are currently available.	Show which group members are still active in the group.	Show the current activities of the group members.
	BUDDY LIST	Show which buddies are currently available.	Show which buddies are still active in the collaborative system.	Show the current activities of the buddies.
	VIRTUAL ME	Show the availability in relation to the virtual identity.	Adapt the representation of the virtual identity in relation to the user's activity.	Show the current activity in relation to the virtual identity.

Use of the Modifier Concept to Increase Richness and Nuance in the Pattern Language

In the P4CMI language, the modifiers AVAILABILITY STATUS, ALIVENESS INDICATOR, and ACTIVITY INDICATOR are described as full design patterns. Though the combination of the patterns, i.e. USER LIST in combination with AVAILABILITY STATUS and ACTIVITY INDICATOR, occurred very often during development projects and appear to be a natural combination of patterns, the involved patterns are not linked via the related patterns sections. Using the modifier design pattern, these valuable combinations are identified and the specific role of the modifier design patterns helps the designers in making design choices based on the pattern language. A revised edition of the pattern language could take that into account. In such cases, we would explicitly describe the identified patterns as modifiers, and thereby reduce the complexity of the pattern language.

The above case study shows that by evaluating pattern sequences and identifying recurring combination of patterns, it is possible to identify valuable best practices. The modifier concept allows pattern language authors to explicitly highlight these best practices. The above three modifiers were identified by evaluating recurring pattern sequences in development projects. These modifiers can be applied to five patterns in the P4CMI language. Thus, various combinations of eight concepts in the pattern language yield a total of 40 possible solutions while adding far fewer new patterns to the language. Introducing the modifier concept to the P4CMI language increases its richness and nuances, while holding combinatorial explosion in check.

During the writing process of the P4CMI language quite a few pattern ideas were skipped as the idea proved not to be mature enough for the inclusion of a new pattern. Reflecting on the writing process, it now becomes clear that some of the immature patterns were finally included as variations of the solution in the danger spot section of several patterns. Using the modifier pattern and explicitly highlighting these variations would have improved the clarity and usability of the pattern language for the users of the P4CMI language.

4   Expert Evaluation

In addition to these cases, we performed an expert evaluation. We mailed the description of the modifier pattern to 13 experts, and asked them four questions to evaluate the modifier design pattern:

1) Do you think the modifier concept is useful in the structuring and authoring of a pattern language? Please, elaborate.
2) Do you envision that using modifiers will, indeed,
   a) increase richness of a pattern language,
   b) improve the structure of a pattern language,
   c) reduce the complexity of a pattern language
3) Can you point to examples of pattern languages in which a similar concept is used, or do you have anecdotes or other experiences in which you could see the modifier concept as a solution?
4) Would you consider using the modifier concept when authoring a (future) pattern language? Please, explain.

Four experts on pattern languages responded to our questionnaire by e-mail. Another five experts responded at a pattern language workshop and four experts who received a write-up of the concept provided qualitative feedback on the merits of the approach. The experts reported the modifier concept to be useful, but not necessarily easy to use. While it might reduce the number of patterns and increase structure, it adds a different level of complexity; the interrelatedness of patterns in the pattern language. Some, therefore, suggest that modifiers should be a concept for advanced pattern users. The experts also suggested that it might be useful if the designers of pattern languages were to designate some patterns as 'basic' design patterns, to further distinguish them from modifiers. This action might imply a choice of what the 'default,' or most preferred solutions were, and which were the variations, which is not likely to be a trivial decision for pattern language authors.

All experts agreed that the modifier concept would increase richness of a pattern language. Capturing modifiers separately will enable the pattern language author to highlight variations of solutions that are used less frequently, without increasing the size of the pattern language.

The concept of a modifier was a concern for some of the experts. Modifiers do not provide a solution by themselves, and yet they are a recurring variation on a solution. This poses the question, are modifiers a kind of pattern if they do not constitute a complete solution? Experts differed on this point. Some indicated that patterns should stand 'on their own' while others indicated that the recurring nature of the modifier solution justifies its status as a design pattern. The structure of a modifier (how to capture it) could be similar to a design pattern; however, emphasis will be on how to combine the modifier with other patterns in the language, while the solution description is likely to be small in size, compared to 'normal' design patterns. However, the modifier does describe a reusable solution to a recurring problem, and therefore is a pattern, it just needs to be combined with other patterns.

Only one of the experts offered an example of a pattern language where modifiers might be useful. Several experts indicated that modifiers are only useful to complex pattern languages, not to simple languages. Several experts pointed out the need for an approach for identifying modifiers and distinguishing them from basic patterns when a community develops and uses a pattern language. Such a decision would require consideration of removing or replacing patterns in the pattern language and so might require a kind of 'editorial board' to evaluate the status and relations of a new pattern with existing patterns in the language.

5   Discussion and Conclusions

We argue in this paper the need for and the value of the modifier concept in pattern languages. The first advantage of the use of modifiers is that modifiers can make a pattern language at once more powerful and more parsimonious. Modifiers make a pattern language more powerful by extending the variety and nuance of the solutions the language. Modifiers make a pattern language more parsimonious by reducing a tendency toward combinatorial explosion of design patterns. While the use of modifiers may not be obvious or necessary in every domain, modifiers may help to both enrich and simplify some pattern languages, while offering a wider variety of useful and deliberate design choices. This will offer the user more insight in ways to combine design patterns and modifiers in the pattern language. Further, it will help the community to capture knowledge on variations, refinements and combinations of design patterns, enabling them to articulate the role of a specific pattern. In this way the modifier concept strengthens the pattern language approach. It offers a way to deal with the open nature of design pattern languages. Patterns can be combined in so many ways, novices might have trouble choosing among design solutions (and even more so when design patterns are not yet identified in a domain). Identifying design patterns and modifiers in the pattern language offers a novice working with patterns more structure and a way to deal with design complexity in a domain.

A second benefit of the modifier is that it improves the structure and overview of the pattern language. Design pattern languages offer a set of interlinked problem-solution combinations. In this sense a pattern language offers novices knowledge in a structure that will help them to store this information in their memory in a more accessible way [24]. Research on cognition has indicated that the availability and inter-relatedness of schema in our memory determines the difference between experts and novices in several ways [25]: An expert, compared to a novice does not have more schema, but larger schema, created through a process called chunking [26]. A second difference is that an expert recognizes patterns of problems from previous experience and combines these in his schema with solution-directions, while novices do not possess such schema and thus have to solve the problem from scratch. This lack of so-phisticated schema causes another difference between novices and experts. Experts categorize their knowledge based on solution models, while novices do not yet see the direct relation between problems and solutions, they can only structure their schema based on similarities in the problem statement [27]. Concluding, an expert, compared to a novice, has better, larger schema that are more automated, more interrelated and therefore more accessible through a better categorization and association with other schema. Furthermore, these expert schema are based on solution models instead of surface structures [25]. The relation between design patterns and schema has been discussed by several researchers [24, 28], and leads to the hypothesis that offering novices a pattern language which is highly interrelated might be slightly more complex, but in the end might help them to quickly learn to think and design as an expert within a given domain. This is an interesting topic for further research.

Further research is also required to evaluate the added value of the use of modifiers from both an expert perspective (authors of pattern languages) and from a user perspective (communities that use design patterns). Initial feedback from both were positive; authors see the value of this concept for their languages and users can give examples of patterns that could be described as modifiers.

Acknowledgements

We thank our shepherd Kristian Elof Sørensen, our peers in the shepherd workshop at EuroPlop, and the anonymous reviewers for the T-Plop issue for their insightful feedback.

References

1. Alexander, C.: The Timeless Way of Building. Oxford University Press, New York (1979)
2. Gamma, E., Helm, R., Johnson, R., Vlissides, J.: Elements of Reusable Object-Oriented Software. Addison-Wesley Publishing Company, Reading (1995)
3. Lukosch, S., Schümmer, T.: Groupware Development Support with Technology Patterns. International Journal of Human Computer Systems 64 (2006)
4. Rising, L.: Design Patterns in Communication Software. Cambridge University Press, Cambridge (2001)

5. Niegemann, H.M., Domagk, S.: ELEN Project Evaluation Report. University of Erfurt, Erfurt (2005)
6. May, D., Taylor, P.: Knowledge Management with Patterns: Developing techniques to improve the process of converting information to knowledge. Communications of the ACM 44, 94–99 (2003)
7. Kolfschoten, G.L., Briggs, R.O., Vreede, G.J., de, J.P.H.M., Appelman, J.H.: Conceptual Foundation of the ThinkLet Concept for Collaboration Engineering. International Journal of Human Computer Science 64, 611–621 (2006)
8. de Vreede, G.J., Briggs, R.O., Kolfschoten, G.L.: ThinkLets: A Pattern Language for Facilitated and Practitioner-Guided Collaboration Processes. International Journal of Computer Applications in Technology 25, 140–154 (2006)
9. Rising, L.: Understanding the Power of Abstraction in Patterns. IEEE Software 24, 46–51 (2007)
10. Noble, J.: Classifying Relationships between Object-Oriented Design Patterns. In: Australian Software Engineering Conference. IEEE Computer Society Press, Los Alamitos (1998)
11. Coplien, J.O., Harrison, N.B.: Organizational Patterns of Agile Software Development. Pearson Prentice Hall, Upper Saddle River (2005)
12. Hvatum, L.B., Simien, T., Cretoiu, A., Hliot, D.: Patterns and Advice for Managing Distributed Product Development Teams. Euro Plop. EuroPlop, Irsee, Germany (2005)
13. Duyne, D.K.v., Landay, J.A., Hong, J.I.: The Design of Sites: Patterns for Creating Winning Web Sites. Prentice Hall PTR, Englewood Cliffs (2006)
14. Briggs, R.O., de Vreede, G.J., Nunamaker jr., J.F.: Collaboration Engineering with ThinkLets to Pursue Sustained Success with Group Support Systems. Journal of Management Information Systems 19, 31–63 (2003)
15. Kolfschoten, G.L., Appelman, J.H., Briggs, R.O., de Vreede, G.J.: Recurring Patterns of Facilitation Interventions in GSS Sessions. In: Hawaii International Conference on System Sciences. IEEE Computer Society Press, Los Alamitos (2004)
16. Kolfschoten, G.L., van Houten, S.P.A.: Predictable Patterns in Group Settings through the use of Rule Based Facilitation Interventions. In: Kersten, G.E., Rios, J. (eds.) Group Decision and Negotiation Conference. Concordia University, Mt Tremblant (2007)
17. Grünbacher, P., Halling, M., Biffl, S., Kitapchi, H., Boehm, B.W.: Integrating Collaborative Processes and Quality Assurance Techniques: Experiences from Requirements Negotiation. Journal of Management Information Systems 20, 9–29 (2004)
18. Valacich, J.S., Jessup, L.M., Dennis, A.R., Nunamaker jr., J.F.: A Conceptual Framework of Anonymity in Group Support Systems. Group Decision and Negotiation 1, 219–241 (1992)
19. Kolfschoten, G.L., Santanen, E.L.: Reconceptualizing Generate ThinkLets: the Role of the Modifier. In: Hawaii International Conference on System Science, IEEE Computer Society Press, Waikoloa (2007)
20. Schümmer, T., Lukosch, S.: Patterns for Computer-Mediated Interaction. John Wiley & Sons Ltd., Chichester (2007)
21. Bikson, T.K., Eveland, J.D.: Groupware implementation: reinvention in the sociotechnical frame. In: ACM Conference on Computer Supported Cooperative Work, pp. 428–437. ACM Press, New York (1996)
22. Schümmer, T., Lukosch, S., Slagter, R.: Using Patterns to Empower End-users - The Oregon Software Development Process for Groupware. International Journal of Cooperative Information Systems 15, 259–288 (2006)

23. Schümmer, T., Lukosch, S.: Structure-Preserving Transformations in Pattern-Driven Groupware Development. International Journal of Computer Applications in Technology 25, 155–166 (2006)

24. Kolfschoten, G.L., Valentin, E., de Vreede, G.J., Verbraeck, A.: Cognitive Load Reduction Through the Use of Building Blocks in the Design of Decision Support Systems. In: Romano Jr., N.C. (ed.) Americas Conference on Information Systems. AIS, Acapulco (2006)

25. Sweller, J.: Cognitive load during problem solving: Effects on learning. Cognitive Science 12, 257–285 (1988)

26. Simon, H.A.: How Big is a Chunk? Science 183, 482–488 (1974)

27. Bjork- Ligon, E., Bjork, R.A. (eds.): Memory Handbook of Perception and Cognition. Academic Press, San Diego (1996)

28. Kohls, C., Scheiter, K.: The relation between design patterns and schema theory. In: Conference on Pattern Languages of Programs, pp. 1–16. ACM, Nashville (2008)

Patterns for Effectively Documenting Frameworks

Ademar Aguiar and Gabriel David

INESC Porto, Departamento de Engenharia Informática,
Faculdade de Engenharia da Universidade do Porto,
Rua Dr. Roberto Frias, 4200-465 Porto, Portugal
{ademar.aguiar,gtd}@fe.up.pt

Abstract. Good design and implementation are necessary but not sufficient pre-requisites for successfully reusing object-oriented frameworks. Although not always recognized, good documentation is crucial for effective framework re-use, and often hard, costly, and tiresome, coming with many issues, especially when we are not aware of the key problems and respective ways of addressing them. Based on existing literature, case studies and lessons learned, the authors have been mining proven solutions to recurrent problems of documenting ob-ject-oriented frameworks, and writing them in pattern form, as patterns are a very effective way of communicating expertise and best practices. This paper presents a small set of patterns addressing problems related to the framework documentation itself, here seen as an autonomous and tangible product inde-pendent of the process used to create it. The patterns aim at helping non-experts on cost-effectively documenting object-oriented frameworks. In concrete, these patterns provide guidance on choosing the kinds of documents to produce, how to relate them, and which contents to include. Although the focus is more on the documents themselves, rather than on the process and tools to produce them, some guidelines are also presented in the paper to help on applying the patterns to a specific framework.

Keywords: Patterns, object-oriented frameworks, documentation.

1 Introduction

Software reuse is the activity of using existing software artifacts in the development of new software systems. Different reuse techniques usually use different software artifacts, differing in scale, abstractness and complexity, which range from concrete source-code components to highly abstract architectures. Firmly in the middle of this range, we find object-oriented frameworks, a powerful technique for large-scale reuse capable of delivering high levels of design and code reuse.

An object-oriented framework can be defined as a reusable, semi-defined applica-tion that can be specialized to produce custom applications. Through design and code reuse, frameworks help developers to achieve higher productivity, shorter time-to-market and improved compatibility and consistency. When combined with components and patterns, frameworks are considered the most promising current technology sup-porting large-scale reuse. Perhaps the best evidence of the power of object-oriented

J. Noble et al. (Eds.): TPLOP II, LNCS 6510, pp. 79–124, 2011.

frameworks is reflected on the well-known success of many examples of popular frameworks, such as: Model-View-Controller (MVC), MacApp, ET++, Microsoft Foundation Classes (MFCs), IBM's SanFrancisco, several parts of Sun's Java Foundation Classes (RMI, AWT, Swing), many implementations of the Object Management Group's (OMG) Common Object Request Broker Architecture (CORBA), Microsoft .NET framewirks, and Apache's frameworks (Cocoon, Struts). Despite the existing difficulties of reusing frameworks, all the above examples of frameworks are playing, directly or indirectly, a very important role in contemporary software development.

Although frameworks promise higher development productivity, shorter time-to-market, and higher quality, these benefits are only gained over time and require up-front investments. Before being able to use a framework successfully, users usually need to spend a lot of effort on understanding its underlying architecture and design principles, and on learning how to customize it. All of this together implies a steep learning curve that can be significantly reduced with good documentation and training material.

This work contributes with a comprehensive set of patterns focusing on problems of documenting frameworks [2][3][4][5], some of the several technical, organizational, and managerial issues that must be well managed in order to employ frameworks effectively.

1.1 Pattern Language

The pattern language for documenting frameworks comprises a set of interdependent patterns that aim at helping developers to adopt a systematic way of solving, or simply becoming aware of, the typical problems they will face when documenting object-oriented frameworks.

The pattern language describes a path commonly followed when documenting a framework, not necessarily from start to end to achieve effective results. In fact, many frameworks are not documented as completely as suggested by the patterns, due to different kinds of usage (white-box or black-box) and different balancing of tradeoffs between cost, quality, detail, and complexity. One of the goals of these patterns is precisely to expose such tradeoffs in each pattern, and to provide practical guidelines on how to balance them to find the best combination of documents, activities and tools to the specific context at hands.

The patterns here presented were mined from existing literature, lessons learned, and expertise on documenting frameworks, including a previous compilation of the authors about framework documentation [1].

This document focuses on patterns closely related to the documentation itself, here seen as an autonomous and tangible product independent of the process used to create it. The patterns provide guidance on choosing the right documents to produce, how to relate them, and which contents to include [2][3][4].

From the framework documentation reader's point of view, the most important issue is on providing accurate task-oriented information, well organized, understandable, and easy to retrieve with search and query facilities.

From the writer's point of view, the key issues include: identifying the documentation needs, selecting the contents, choosing the best representation for the contents, and organizing the contents adequately, so that the documentation results of good quality, valuable for the target audience, while easy to produce and maintain.

1.2   Pattern Thumbnails

To describe the patterns, we started from the Christopher Alexander's pattern form [6] and adapted it to include the following sections: Name, Context, Problem, Forces, Solution, Examples, and Known Uses.

Before starting detailing each pattern, we will overview the patterns included in this document by summarizing their intents. Figure 1 shows all the patterns and their relationships.

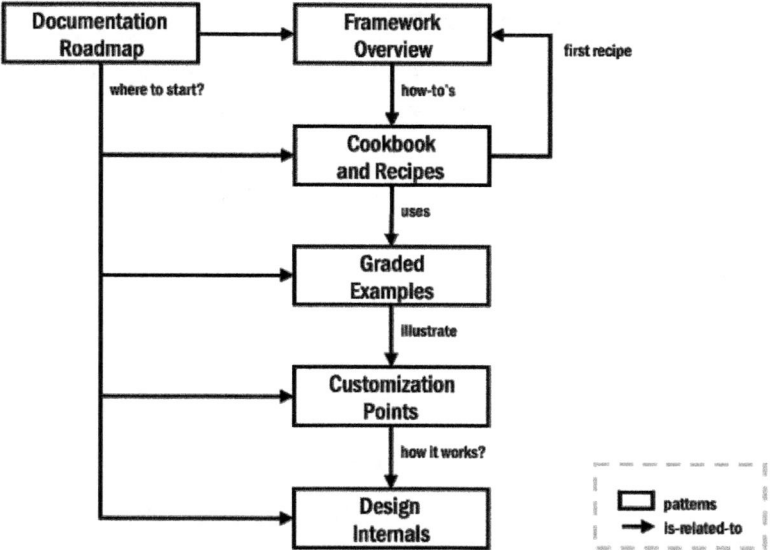

Fig. 1. Documentation patterns and their relationships

DOCUMENTATION ROADMAP helps on deciding what to include in the documentation overview to provide readers of different audiences with useful and effective hints on what to read to acquire the knowledge they are looking for.

FRAMEWORK OVERVIEW suggests providing introductory information, in the form of a framework overview, briefly describing the domain, the scope of the framework, and the flexibility offered, because contextual information about the framework is the first kind of information that a framework user needs.

COOKBOOK & RECIPES explains how to provide readers with information that explain how-to-use the framework to solve specific problems of application development, and how to combine this prescriptive information with small amounts of descriptive information to help users on understanding what they are doing.

GRADED EXAMPLES describes how to provide and organize example applications constructed with the framework and how to cross-reference them with the other kinds of artefacts (cookbooks, patterns, and source code).

CUSTOMIZABLE POINTS describes how to provide readers with task-oriented information with more precision and more design detail than cookbooks and recipes, so that readers can quickly identify the customizable points of the framework (hot-spots) and to understand how they are supported (hooks).

DESIGN INTERNALS explains how to provide detailed information about what can be adapted and how the adaptation is supported, by referring the patterns that are used in its implementation and where they are instantiated.

1.3 Pattern-Based Documentation Process

To produce the documentation, there is a life cycle typically organized in five basic activities: configuration, production, organization, usage, and maintenance (Figure 2). Each activity poses their specific problems, closely related to the activities, roles and tools needed to cost-effectively produce the documents [5].

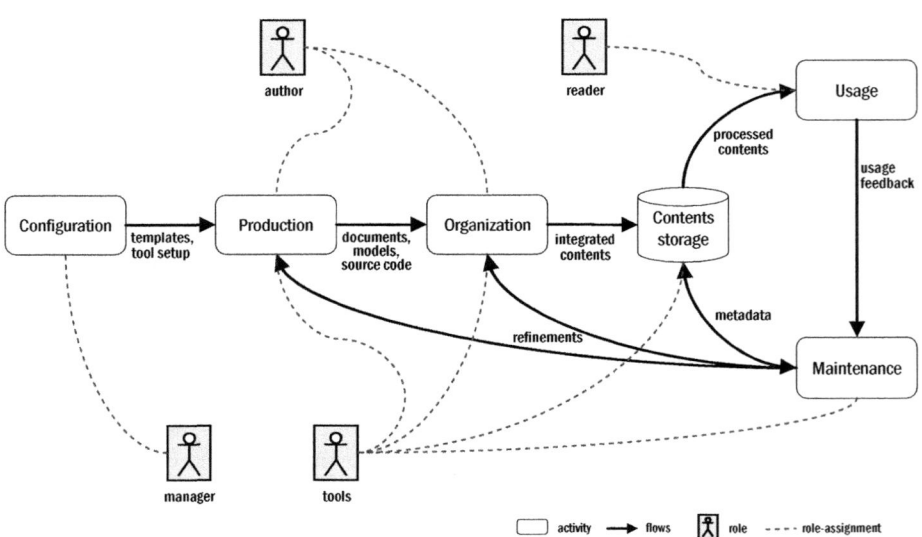

Fig. 2. Typical activities and roles of documenting frameworks

Examples of these problems are: identifying the target audiences, organizing and creating documents, linking related documents, preserving the semantic consistency of duplicated contents, choosing the right documentation tools, and publishing the documents.

Although implicit in the problem-solution pairs of each pattern, there is a very simple method subjacent in all patterns that promote a systematic approach for documenting frameworks. The method aims at being flexible, almost neutral, and easy to adapt to different projects and development environments.

Process Goals

The key goals of the process underlying the application of these patterns are the following:

- **To provide easy-to-follow guidelines.** Although guidelines cannot guarantee quality documentation, they help improve individual quality attributes in a measurable and repeatable way. The goal is to provide some guidelines in the solution section of the patterns, so that writers, especially novices, can find guidance when documenting a framework.
- **To be cost-effective.** To be useful in practice, the cost of documentation must not significantly outweigh its benefits. The goal is to help writers on finding the right balance of the forces, explicitly mentioned in each pattern, for their specific situations.
- **To be user-centered.** Documentation is a means to communicate knowledge to the users, not an end. The goal is to center the process on the user: to analyze user's needs, to design the documentation, to write, test, and refine, until it is ready for usage. The guidelines presented in pattern form suggest a problem-driven approach, thus user-oriented.
- **To support reuse.** To improve documentation productivity, it is important to reuse previous knowledge and artifacts. The goal is to promote the reuse of artifacts (templates, conventions, rules, etc.) and processes (guidelines, tools, integrations). These patterns do not impose any specific template or guideline, but their systematic application helps on finding commonalities that can lead to

Following these goals, a few roles, techniques, activities, and guidelines were defined and embedded in the patterns.

Roles

The documentation is written by different kinds of people, in different phases of the process, which must cooperate and collaborate during the documentation process. There are three roles suggested by the patterns:

- **Technical writers** are responsible to structure, guide, review, and conclude the documentation; this role is especially important for patterns DOCUMEN-TATION ROADMAP, FRAMEWORK OVERVIEW, and COOKBOOK & RECIPES;
- **Developers** are responsible for content creation mostly during development; this role is especially important for patterns GRADED EXAMPLES, CUSTOM-IZABLE POINTS, and DESIGN INTERNALS;
- **Documentation managers** are responsible for configuring and maintaining the documentation base; this role is equally important for all patterns.

Activities

Since the production of framework documentation is closely related with framework design and usage, ideally, these activities should be done in parallel, possibly side-by-side, if we want to obtain documentation that is understandable, consistent, and easy-to-maintain. The key activities suggested by the patterns are the following:

- **configuration** of the documentation base; this activity is present in all patterns but more explicit in **DOCUMENTATION ROADMAP**;
- **creation and cross-referencing** of the various kinds of contents; this activity is present in all patterns;
- **normalization, integration and storage** of contents; this activity is not considered in the patterns, since it is orthogonal to all of them and would constrain its flexibility;
- **publishing and presentation** of contents to target audiences; this activity is not considered in the patterns, for the same reason as above.

After a configuration phase, the production of framework documentation starts with the creation of the various kinds of contents, and their cross-referencing. Upon creation, the different kinds of contents are normalized, integrated and stored in a repository from where they will be retrieved, transformed, published and presented to target audiences.

What to write	Why	By who	To whom	When
Framework documentation				
Framework overview	to give an overview of the framework: domain, customizations, documentation	writer, developer	all audiences	first release
Cookbooks, recipes	to explain how to use the framework: the points of customization and the steps required to perform	developer, writer	framework users	development
Examples	to provide concrete examples of usage of the framework	developer	framework users	development
Hot spot	to provide information about the points of the framework that accept customization	developer	framework users, framework developers, framework maintainers	development
Hook	to provide detailed design information about how to customize the framework in a specific point of flexility	developer	framework users, framework developers, framework maintainers	development
Patterns	to provide design information about how the framework works to offer a specific functionality: classes, methods, roles, collaborations	developer, writer	framework users, framework developers, framework maintainers	design
Pattern instances	to provide detailed design information about how the framework was implemented to offer the flexibility and extensibility	developer	framework users, framework developers, framework maintainers	development

Fig. 3. Typical authors for the different types of documents

Guidelines

In addition to the roles and activities presented above, the patterns implicitly provide some guidelines to help writers on effectively producing good quality framework documentation.

The table in Figure 3 lists the major types of documents suggested by the patterns and provides answers to the why's, who's and when's of each type of document. Considering a particular type of document, the meaning of each column of the table is the following:

- **why**, defines its purpose, the goal that it helps to achieve;
- by **who**, defines who are the authors typically responsible for writing it;
- to **whom**, defines who benefits from it;
- **when**, defines the development phase considered the best for writing it.

The list is not exhaustive and is presented only as indicative information, not prescriptive.

1.4 Pattern Application: A Typical Sequence

To better illustrate when and how the patterns above can be applied, let's consider a typical case of an existing framework about which there isn't any kind of information other than its source code.

When new application developers, other than the original framework developers, start trying to reuse the framework, the need for written information becomes evident and the framework team decides to start documenting the framework.

One of the first documents to write is usually for explaining the purpose of the framework and its application domain (pattern **FRAMEWORK OVERVIEW**).

In a second moment, it is important to provide new framework users with concrete examples, from simple to complex ones, which can be used, understood, and learnt by framework users (pattern **GRADED EXAMPLES**).

As documentation grows, the need to keep it organized and easy to access usually leads to the creation of a documentation overview capable of guiding readers directly to the information they look for (pattern **DOCUMENTATION ROADMAP**).

Additional documents can then be written, as needed, to explain how to do the most typical customizations of the framework, in a very pragmatic and prescriptive way (pattern **COOKBOOK & RECIPES**).

When more detailed information is required about the framework's configuration points and their implementation, specialized documentation should be provided at a level of abstraction above the source code. This can be provided either from an external point of view (pattern **CUSTOMIZABLE POINTS**), enumerating all known framework points specifically designed to support customization, or from an internal perspective (pattern **DESIGN INTERNALS**), revealing as much as possible its design internals, most notable the design tradeoffs and decisions made.

The sequence of pattern instantiation above outlined is probably the most common in agile projects, which are very restrictive with documentation effort, suggesting that documentation should be lean and lightweight. In agile projects, documentation is mostly produced collaboratively, when needed, and published publicly, using simple tools.

Other sequences are obviously possible, and should be defined according to the project needs. Independently of the sequence followed, these patterns help on adopting a systematic approach to document frameworks, driven by the specific documentation needs at hands, and accommodate well to different project documentation constraints and needs: completeness, time, cost, target audience, and process discipline and agility.

1.5 Paper Outline

After this introduction to the overall pattern language and its underlying concepts, Section 2 presents a concise review of the key issues of documenting frameworks and related work. The six patterns are then described in the following sections. To illustrate the patterns, examples and known uses are described using different well-known frameworks: JUnit, as a small example; and Java Foundation Classes, .NET, and Eclipse as examples of large frameworks. Although several other frameworks could be used for this purpose, since the patterns are present in several other frameworks, the criteria were to select frameworks widely available, highly popular, and with different budgets. The paper concludes with final considerations about the contribution of these patterns.

2   Key Issues of Documenting Frameworks

By nature, frameworks are much more difficult to document than object-oriented applications or class libraries, being its generativity aspect one of the major reasons. Frameworks are a software product specifically built to create other software products, and therefore they are designed to be flexible and extensible, which makes them hard to explain how to use, and how they work, especially to new users.

There are several issues associated with framework documentation, both technical and non-technical [1] (Figure 4). They include fundamental issues of technical documentation, such as quality assessment, common issues of software documentation, and several issues specific to framework documentation, related with the documentation product itself, the process used to create it, and the tools used to support the process.

General documentation issues	
Technical	Quality assessment
Software	semantic consistency, appropriate documentation environments, knowledge acquisition, programmer's attitude
Framework-specific documentation issues	
Product	Combining prescriptive and descriptive information, managing consistency and redundancy, good organization of contents, graded presentation of contents, several entry points and traversal paths, multiple views and outputs, contents integration
Process	Lack of standards, guidelines, cost, user-centered process, documentation reuse
Tools	Authoring tools, contents synchronization, extraction tools, browse and retrieval facilities

Fig. 4. Enumeration of framework documentation issues [1]

2.1 Quality Assessment Issues

Good quality technical documentation is the ultimate goal of documentation writers, and what system users definitely look for. But to produce good quality documentation comes with many issues, being perhaps the first obstacle the difficulty of defining and assessing its quality.

The book *Producing Quality Technical Information* (PQTI) [31] contain one of the earliest comprehensive discussions about the multidimensional nature of quality documentation. In the revised edition of PQTI, *Developing Quality Technical Information* (DQTI) [30], these dimensions are refined and expanded to nine dimensions organized into three overriding categories: easy to use, easy to understand, and easy to find (Figure 5). DQTI is targeted for general use and already takes in account online information (help, tutorials, etc.).

Quality dimension	Description
Easy to Use	
Task Orientation	Helps users complete tasks related to their work by using the product.
Accuracy	Contains no mistakes or errors, truthful and factual.
Completeness	Includes all essential parts (but only these parts).
Easy to Understand	
Clarity	Contains no ambiguity or obscurity.
Concreteness	Contains no abstractions; including appropriate examples, scenarios, and metaphors.
Style	Uses correct and appropriate writing conventions and word choice.
Easy to Find	
Organization	Organizes material coherently in a way that makes sense to the user.
Retrievability	Presents information in a way that lets users find information quickly and easily.
Visual Effectiveness	Uses layout, illustrations, color, type, icons, and other graphical devices to enhance meaning and attractiveness.

Fig. 5. Quality dimensions for technical information [30]

When addressing problems of software documentation, it is important to be aware of the general issues of technical documentation. However, they are well beyond the scope of the specific topic of framework documentation.

2.2 Software Documentation Issues

Although not always recognized, documentation plays a central role in software development. Most of the development effort is spent on formalizing information, that is, on reading and understanding requirements, informal specifications, drawings, reports, memos, electronic messages, and other informal documents, in order to produce formal documents, such as source code files, models and specifications.

The general issues associated with software documentation become even more important in the context of reusable assets, such as frameworks. These issues include the preservation of the semantic consistency between different documents (such as informal documents and code), the lack of appropriate documentation environments, the knowledge acquisition problem, and the attitude problem of developers in respect to the priorities of documentation. All these issues have a strong impact on the cost of producing, evolving, and maintaining software documentation.

2.3 Product Issues

The first category of framework documentation issues is related with the documentation itself, seen as an autonomous and tangible product independent of the process used to create it.

The difficulties more specific to framework documentation, as considered by the authors, are related with the following attributes: task-orientation, organization, retrievability, accuracy, and visual effectiveness.

From an external perspective, the reader's point of view, the most important issues are on providing accurate task-oriented information, well organized, understandable, and easy to retrieve with the help of search and querying facilities. From an internal perspective, the writer's point of view, the key issues are on selecting the contents to include, on choosing the best representation for the contents, and on organizing the contents adequately, so that the documentation results of good quality, and easy to produce and maintain. Here is a quick overview of such issues [1]:

- **Combining prescriptive and descriptive information.** Framework users want practical information (prescriptive information, concrete examples), explaining how-to-use the framework. However, related descriptive information (patterns, contracts, etc.) is also important to be available, to explain how the framework works.
- **Managing consistency and redundancy.** Readers' comprehension is fast when information is provided with accuracy, without inconsistencies between their different kinds of contents (text, source code, models).
- **Good organization of contents.** The external organization is how the contents fit together, as perceived by the reader. A good and easy to understand organization of information helps readers be more effective when using the documentation, because the perceived organization enables them to predict the information they will find in certain parts of the documentation.
- **Graded presentation of contents.** Contents must be organized in a graded, or spiral way, emphasizing main points first, and subordinating secondary points for later. This helps minimize the amount of information needed to read and understand at once.
- **Several entry points and traversal paths.** Documentation readers should be able to follow their preferred learning strategy, such as hierarchical-based or example-based strategies. Due to the potential huge amount of contents, it is important that readers are able to locate framework parts starting from different documentation entry points (e.g. overviews, examples, patterns, etc.).
- **Multiple views and outputs.** The documentation must be configurable to provide a variety of document views (static, dynamic, internal, external, etc.) to effectively support the several kinds of tasks that different people, from different audiences, and with varying levels of experience want to perform.

- **Contents integration.** The internal organization is how the contents are tied together during production. All kinds of framework documents should be easy to integrate in a unified whole, to be easy to share, manage and interchange. In particular, documents must be conveniently integrated with the program code, in order to guarantee semantic consistency and to be easy to navigate from code to documents and vice-versa.

2.4 Process Issues

When documenting a framework, besides deciding *what* to document, the main issues are relative to the documentation process itself: *when* to document, *who* should be responsible for writing particular documentation contents, and *how* to combine and organize the overall documentation contents in order to achieve good quality.

To be useful, framework documentation must include a lot of contents, gathered from different types of documents, at different moments of the development lifecycle, and produced by different kinds of people. To be cost-effective, the production of documentation must follow a well-defined process capable of orchestrating all participants, and promoting their cooperation.

Although there exists a set of documentation practices commonly accepted as useful for documenting frameworks, such as cookbooks, patterns, and examples, processes for documenting frameworks are still missing. The lack of well-defined processes is one of the most important issues of framework documentation processes. Here is a quick overview of such issues [1]:

- **Lack of standards.** The combination of patterns, hooks, hot spots, examples, and architectural illustrations, has proven to be very effective. However, the combination of different kinds of documents may become very difficult and expensive, both to produce and to maintain, due to the several setup efforts and the probable overlap, unless there is a commonly accepted method for documenting frameworks, or a standard for framework documentation, or at least, an infrastructure to help produce, combine and present the contents of framework documentation.
- **Guidelines.** Although checklists, requirements, and guidelines for writing documentation cannot guarantee the development of quality documentation, they help improve individual quality attributes in a measurable and repeatable way, and therefore contribute to improve the overall documentation quality. It is important to get from documentation experts such checklists and guidelines, so that writers, especially novices, can find guidance when documenting a framework.
- **Cost.** To be useful in practice, the cost of documentation must not significantly outweigh its benefits. Especially during framework maintenance, it is very important that the documentation is inexpensive and easy to evolve; otherwise it won't be updated at all, becoming inconsistent, and thus negating the benefits of producing framework documentation.
- **User-centered process.** In order to fine-tune the documentation to the needs of framework users, it is important to follow a user-centered documentation

process, monitoring the usage, getting user feedback, and then reflect the observations in future documentation releases.

- **Documentation reuse.** To improve documentation productivity, it should be reusable, thus allowing extending and modifying it, without making any changes to the original documentation. Documentation reuse can be achieved through reuse of artifacts (templates, conventions, rules, etc.) or reuse of process (guidelines, tools, integrations).

2.5 Tools Issues

One of the reasons for not documenting adequately is the lack of convenient tools supporting rich representations of the developer's mental information. With the goal of ensuring quality and reducing the typically high costs associated with the production and maintenance of framework documentation, it is mandatory to automate the process the best as possible, while retaining the process flexible and easy to adapt to different developers and environments. Examples of activities that would significantly benefit from automation are described below.

- Authoring tools. Attractive, interoperable, and easy to use tools for assisting writers during production and maintenance of documentation would be an important incentive for more and better documentation. The interoperability of authoring tools with development environments is both a standardization and technical issue.
- Synchronization of contents. The usage of tools or automatic mechanisms to synchronize source code, models, and documents is crucial for preserving the consistency between all the contents, especially in the presence of redundancy. Such synchronization would enable to keep design specifications always updated, that is, "alive", thus motivating for the importance of documenting while developing, instead of documenting after developing.
- Extraction tools. To reduce the effort of producing and using the documentation it is sometimes desirable to automatically produce pre-defined views through reverse engineering of formalized software artifacts, such as, source code, models, or formal specifications. Trivial examples are the generation of UML models directly from source code, or the reverse, currently supported in several tools, such as Borland's Together [Borland, 2003], and IBM's Eclipse [Eclipse, 2003]. More sophisticated automation examples include the identification and classification of the hot spots of a framework, or the mining of patterns (or meta-patterns) instantiated in a framework implementation.
- Browse and retrieval facilities. Due to the usual big amount of information contained in framework documentation, it is important to provide readers with good browsing and retrieval facilities, so that the reader don't become lost in the documentation. Such facilities include selection, filtering, searching, querying, navigation, and history mechanisms (automatic or user defined).

All the issues mentioned above are potential sources of complications to document frameworks that may result in powerful frameworks not being reused (i.e. being wasted) due to the difficulty of understanding them. Many of these issues are interdependent and require proper balancing in order to find effective solutions. Two of these tradeoffs include usage with design information, and prescriptive with descriptive information.

2.6 Usage vs. Design Information

Using a framework and understanding how it works are issues that depend on each other. Framework usage documentation, i.e. documentation describing how a framework is supposed to be used, needs to cover both ways of using a framework: as a black-box system, by simply connecting components, or as a white-box system, by providing extensions to the framework [1].

Much of the work on framework documentation has focused more on ways of representing the design and architecture of frameworks, and less on defining effective ways of helping new users on quickly learning how to use a framework.

One of the reasons for such discrepancy in research effort is perhaps the fact that framework design documentation challenges the capabilities provided by object-oriented design methods and existing software documentation techniques. The design of a framework is usually complex, involving abstract classes and complex object collaborations, thus being best documented with the help of abstractions higher than classes, such as design patterns and role models. In addition, while in software documentation it is possible to clearly separate usage documentation (external view) from system documentation (internal view), with frameworks such separation needs to be fuzzy, as one way of using a framework is by extending it, a kind of usage that requires knowledge about the framework internals [1].

Another possible reason for the discrepancy in framework documentation research effort is that the issues of designing effective user-oriented documentation are typically investigated in the more general fields of technical documentation and computer documentation. In these fields a lot of research is carried on designing usable and understandable task-oriented documentation, which effectively can help users in doing their job, instead of communicating how the system works.

When documenting a software product, we often assume that a good product can be used without knowing how it works, and therefore we clearly separate the user documentation from the system documentation because they have different audiences.

But frameworks are different. The majority of frameworks can be used both as a black-box product and as a white-box product [1]. Therefore, framework usage documentation must mix information both from typical user documentation and system documentation, a situation that poses integration and organization difficulties.

Ralph Johnson authored with other colleagues the first important papers about frameworks [33][34][31][13]. However, Fayad, Johnson, and Schmidt author the most complete source of information about object-oriented frameworks technology, in a set of three volumes that compiles several articles and chapters from different authors [24][25][23]. Older work can be found in Taligent's publications [44][19].

2.7 Prescriptive vs. Descriptive Information

In the article "Documenting frameworks using patterns" [31] Johnson describes a documentation technique that organizes patterns in a pattern language, in a similar way that recipes are organized in a cookbook. Each pattern describes a recurrent problem in the problem domain covered by the framework, and then describes how to solve that problem.

The primary goal of Johnson's patterns is to teach how to use the framework, and then to complement the task-oriented information with explanations about how the framework works, for those willing to know the details. This documentation technique is an attempt to combine prescriptive information (how-to-do) with descriptive information (how-it-works) in order to result effective for new framework users. The perfect balance between these two kinds of information is difficult to fine-tune to a large and heterogeneous audience, because it depends on the context of use, on the user's experience, and on user goals. To be equally effective for different framework users, the balance would require dynamic adjustment, or otherwise, to be intentionally set by the user.

Besides Johnson's work, other different techniques and styles were proposed, both prescriptive (cookbooks, recipes, etc.) and descriptive (design patterns, meta-patterns, architectural models, etc.), as previously described.

Greg Butler's work on framework documentation is perhaps the most complete and comprehensive existing theoretical work, in the opinion of the authors. Butler introduces the concept of reuse cases to catalog the properties of the existing documenting approaches [15]. Butler et al. define the concept of documentation primitive, an elementary unit of documentation, and define a "task-oriented framework for framework documentation" that relates documentation approaches with documentation primitives [16]. Butler also suggests combining a framework overview with examples, and a cookbook with recipes organized in a graded or spiral way. More descriptive information, such as contracts, architecture, or design patterns, might be also available, and accessible as related material. The work of Butler was used as a starting point for the underlying research of these patterns.

Research and experience have proved the effectiveness of some techniques even when used in isolation, namely: cookbooks in [35], patterns [31], and examples. Despite these empirical results, evidence suggests that framework documentation benefits from a combination of techniques in order to deliver complete reference information, detailed design information, effective usage information, and to result easy to use, easy to understand, and easy to find. This evidence is supported by some empirical investigation [36][35].

Meusel et al. [40] propose a model to structure framework documentation that integrates patterns, hypertext, program-understanding tools, and formal approaches into a single structure that is manipulated to address three different kinds of reuse: selecting, using, and extending a framework. The model is based on the pyramid principle and organizes the documentation into three levels of abstraction, one level for each different kind of reuse. The model supports both top-down and bottom-up learning strategies. The article doesn't mention if and how the consistency between source code and documents is achieved, and how the production of the documentation weaves in the development life cycle.

In practice, the lack of standards, common formats, and tools makes the combination of different kinds of documents difficult and expensive both to produce and maintain, due to the difficulties of managing the redundancy introduced, and ensuring its consistency. This concern with consistency is mentioned but not addressed in related work, with the exception of Demeyer et al [20] that reports on the use of open hypermedia systems to keep framework cookbooks up-to-date and consistent with framework source code.

3 Pattern DOCUMENTATION ROADMAP

To completely satisfy all audiences and requirements, the documentation of a framework typically includes a lot of information, organized in different types of documents, namely framework overviews, examples of applications, cookbooks and recipes, design patterns, and reference manuals. These documents provide multiple views over the framework (static, dynamic, external, internal) at different levels of abstraction (architecture, design, implementation), which altogether help to grasp all kinds of information that readers may want to look for in framework documentation.

Problem

The complex web of documents and contents provided with a framework must be organized and presented in a simple manner to the different audiences, so that the readers don't become overwhelmed or lost when using the documentation. In other words, the overall documentation must be easy to use by all kinds of readers, so that each individual reader can quickly acquire the strict degree of understanding she needs to accomplish her particular engineering task (reuse, maintenance or evolution).

How to help readers on quickly finding in the overall documentation their way to the information they need?

Forces

- **Different audiences.** Readers of different audiences have different needs and interests that must be addressed by the documentation.
- **Different kinds of reuse.** A framework can be reused in different ways, each requiring different levels of knowledge about the structure and behavior of the framework, and therefore pose different demands on the documentation.
- **Easy-to-use.** Despite its inherent potential complexity, the documentation must result easy-to-use.

Solution

Start by providing a roadmap for the overall documentation, one that reveals its organization, how the pieces of information fit together, and that elucidates readers of different audiences about the main entry points and the paths in the documentation that may drive them quickly to the information they are looking for, especially at their first contact.

The roadmap would help both when navigating top-down, from a main entry point of the documentation to concrete topics and subtopics, and when navigating bottom-up from a small piece of information to a bigger one to try to identify it as part of a whole, still unknown in a first contact.

To be effective, a documentation roadmap for a framework should be written in a task-oriented manner and to include the following aids:

- topics organized by audience, kind of task, and order of use, to help readers of different audiences quickly retrieval of the information they need to accomplish the tasks they have in mind;

- emphasis of the main entry points and subordination of the secondary ones, to improve visual effectiveness;

- overview of topics conveying how subtopics are related, to support non-linear readings;

- transitions and links to topics, and from them to the roadmap again, to improve the overall navigability around the roadmap.

Although all the above mentioned aids are important to include, in fact, the optimal level of importance assigned to each one depends on several factors: the *framework* being documented, which *audiences* are you willing to address in the overall documentation, which *kinds of reuse* to support explicitly in the documentation, and which *tasks* to emphasize and subordinate.

Independently of how these factors are balanced, the roadmap should be easy to use, easy to understand, well organized, and visually effective, a set of quality characteristics that suggest not to include everything in the roadmap, but only the entry points and topics more relevant for the most important tasks of the target audiences.

Examples

JUnit. The JUnit framework [9] provides a very simple documentation roadmap, where the audiences, kinds of reuse and tasks are implicitly mentioned in the names of the entry points in the documentation and their respective descriptions (Figure 6).

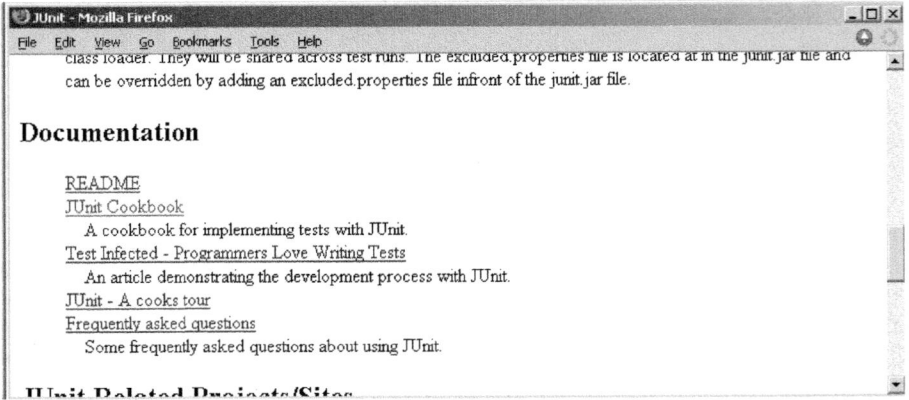

Fig. 6. Example of a very simple documentation roadmap delivered with JUnit

The audiences addressed can be implicitly identified as the following:

- *first-time users*, which will probably be attracted by the "JUnit Cookbook" entry;
- *selectors* and *common users*, by the "Test Infected - Programmers Love Writing Tests" entry;
- and *framework developers*, by the "JUnit - A cooks tour" entry.

The kinds of reuse clearly expressed in this roadmap are:

- *instantiating*, by the "JUnit Cookbook" entry;
- *selecting* and *instantiating*, by the "Test Infected - Programmers Love Writing Tests" entry;
- and *mining*, by the "JUnit - A cooks tour" entry.

Finally, the tasks mentioned are simply *how to implement tests*.

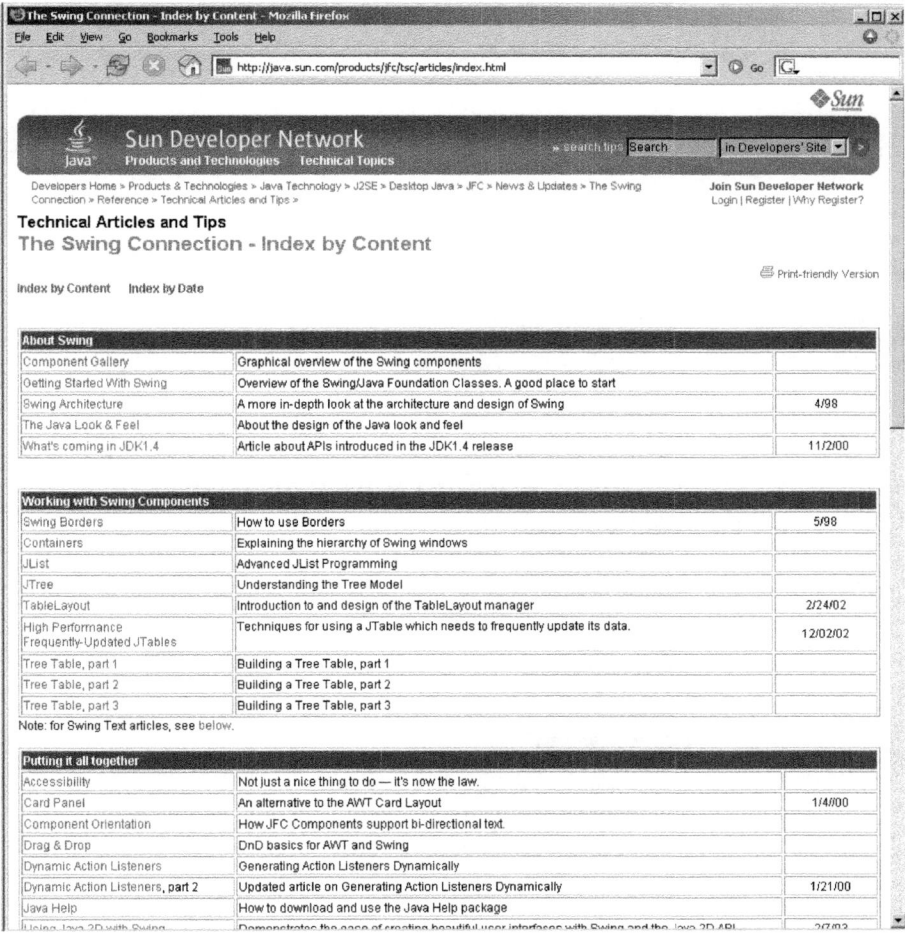

Fig. 7. Example of the complex documentation roadmap for JFC/Swing framework

This roadmap reflects the simplicity of the JUnit's framework itself, the intent of the writers on making the documentation simple and short, by documenting the main usage task of JUnit: to write tests.

Swing. The Sun's JFC/Swing framework [20] is a popular example of a large framework for which exists a lot of documentation.

In part due to its large dimension and vast diversity of possible tasks when reusing Swing, be it black-box or white-box reuse, the roadmap is split along several documents, according to the kind of audience and reuse tasks.

Figure 7 presents "The Swing Connection - Index by Content", which is the document of Swing that mostly resembles a framework documentation roadmap.

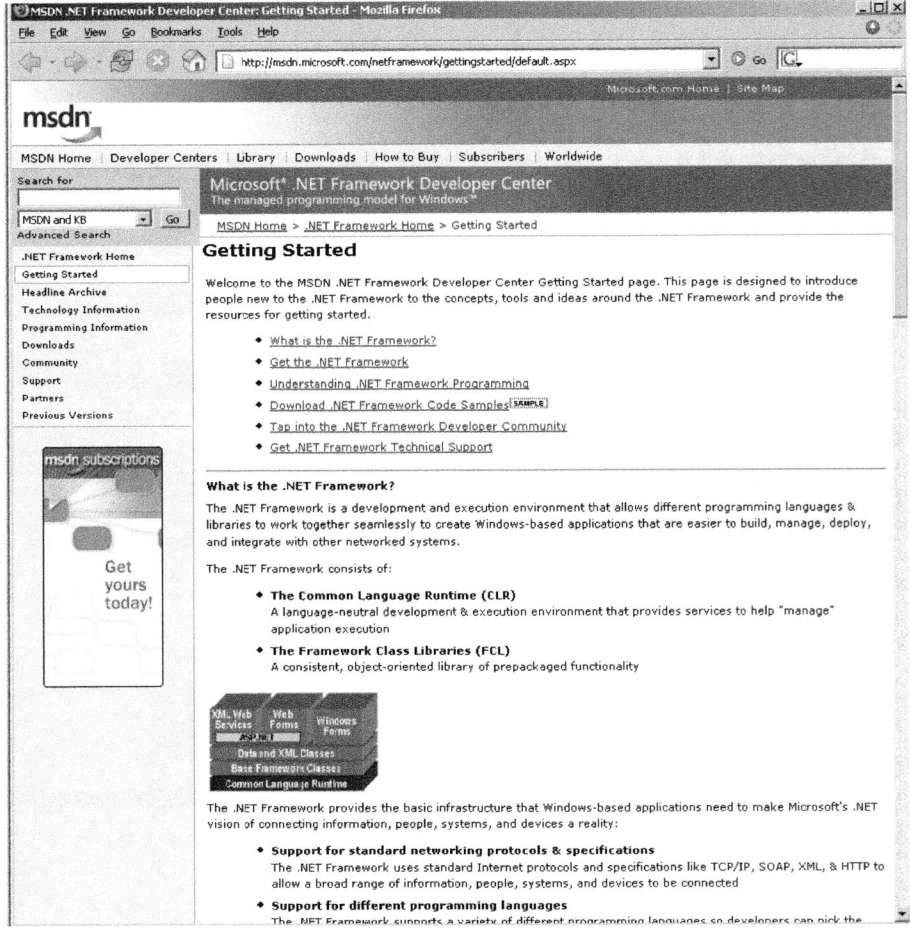

Fig. 8. Example of the documentation roadmap for the .NET framework

.NET. The Microsoft's .NET framework is another popular example of a very large framework for which also exists a lot of documentation.

For this framework there exists a documentation roadmap that clearly addresses different audiences and different kinds of reuse, from where the reader is driven to other documents more specific to the kind of reuse selected with more detailed about the tasks possible with the framework.

Figure 8 presents the "Getting Started" document, which is intended to first-time (re)users, a secondary document accessible from the right-hand side menu that contains the main entry points to the documentation, organized by kind of audience.

4   Pattern FRAMEWORK OVERVIEW

To be effective, the documentation of a framework must include information that explains the purpose of the framework, how to use it, and how it is designed and implemented [39][16].

Problem

In addition to different purposes, the documentation of a framework must also meet the needs of different categories of software engineers involved in framework-based application development, playing different roles (framework selectors, application developers, framework developers, framework maintainers, and developers of other frameworks [15]), having varying levels of experience, and therefore requiring different kinds of information.

> **How to help readers on getting a quick, but precise, first impression of a new framework?**

Forces

- **Different audiences.** In a first contact, the most important kinds of readers to consider are framework selectors, someone who is responsible for deciding which frameworks to use in a project, and new framework users, developers without previous knowledge or experience with the framework [1]. The first kind of information that a new framework user looks for is contextual information. Framework selectors will look for a short description of the framework's purpose, the domain covered, and an explanation of its most important features, ideally illustrated with examples.
- **Completeness.** The readers appreciate complete information, i.e. that all of the required information is available. Completeness implies that all of the relevant information is covered in enough detail, but only the necessary, and that all the promised information is included. But completeness depends on the reader's point of view, and therefore requires knowing the audience and the tasks the documentation should support [30].
- **Easy-to-understand.** Information that is clear, concrete, and written using an appropriate style is usually easy to understand the first time. Clarity (especially

conciseness) often conflicts with completeness (especially relevance and too much information), requiring a good knowledge about *what* readers need to know and *when* they need to know it [30]. Concrete examples help readers on understanding what they are learning because they map abstract concepts to concrete things, which readers can see or manipulate.

Solution

Provide an introductory document, in the form of a framework overview, that describes the domain covered by the framework in a clear way, i.e. the application domain and the range of solutions for which the framework was designed and is applicable.

In addition, a framework overview usually defines the common vocabulary of the problem domain of the framework. It clearly delineates what is covered by the framework and what is not, as well as, what is fixed and what is flexible in the framework. An effective way of communicating this information consists on presenting the basic vocabulary of the problem domain illustrated with a rich set of concrete application examples.

This information is of great value for potential users especially during the selection phase because it helps them to evaluate the appropriateness of the framework for the application at hands, and thus fundaments the selection, or rejection.

In a framework overview, it is common practice to refer or review examples, from simple to complex ones (pattern GRADED EXAMPLES), and to refer or include an overview of all the documentation (pattern DOCUMENTATION ROADMAP). A framework overview is often the first recipe in a cookbook (pattern COOKBOOK & RECIPES).

Examples

JUnit. The framework overview that accompanies JUnit is represented in Figure 9. It was extracted from the document "Frequently Asked Questions (FAQ)" [16], which, from all the documents delivered with the JUnit's framework, is the one that most clearly presents the information typical of a framework overview, despite its placement in a FAQ not being evident in a first contact with the documentation.

Although not being a good exemplar of a framework overview, it contains its most basic ingredients (the domain covered, the features, and an overview of the documentation), and thus it reasonably fulfils the requirements of a framework overview.

The biggest problem with the JUnit's framework overview is that it is not easy to find in a first look at the documentation and is not complete. It is however, easy to understand, what is also very important.

Swing. The framework overview of JFC/Swing is provided in the Sun's tutorial "Creating a GUI with JFC/Swing", lesson "Getting Started with Swing", topic "About the JFC and Swing" (Figure 10).

This framework overview clearly describes the domain covered by the JFC/Swing and its main features. Although, the customizations possible with the framework are described textually in the overview, they are not linked to the concrete examples of applications included in the documentation in other lessons of the tutorial, both visual and source code examples.

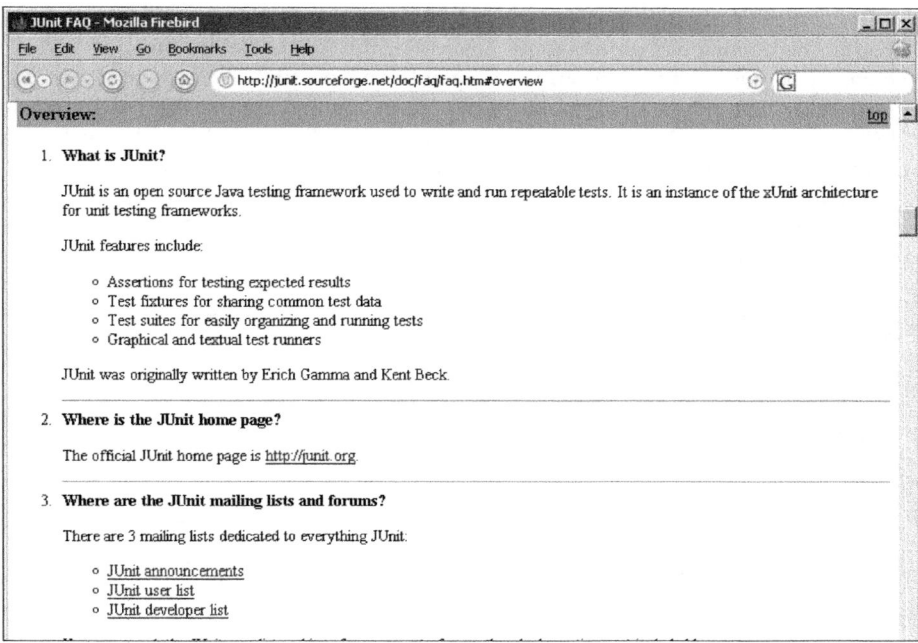

Fig. 9. Example of the framework overview delivered with JUnit

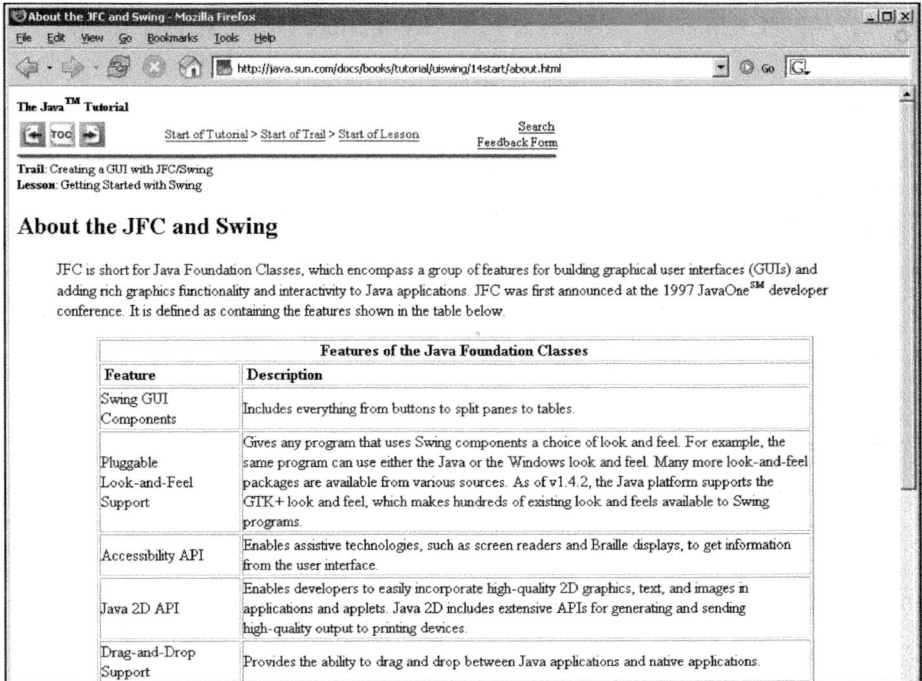

Fig. 10. Example of the framework overview provided for JFC/Swing

Being the JFC/Swing framework so well-known, this placement of the overview so deep in the documentation hierarchy, instead at the top, to be easy to find in a first contact with the documentation, is acceptable and possibly even more convenient, considering that only a small minority of readers are expected to need to learn what JFC/Swing is about. What most readers would need to learn is *what* and *how* they can customize in JFC/Swing to create the GUI they have in mind.

The contents and organization of this framework overview reflects the importance of knowing well the audience and the tasks more likely to need support from the documentation.

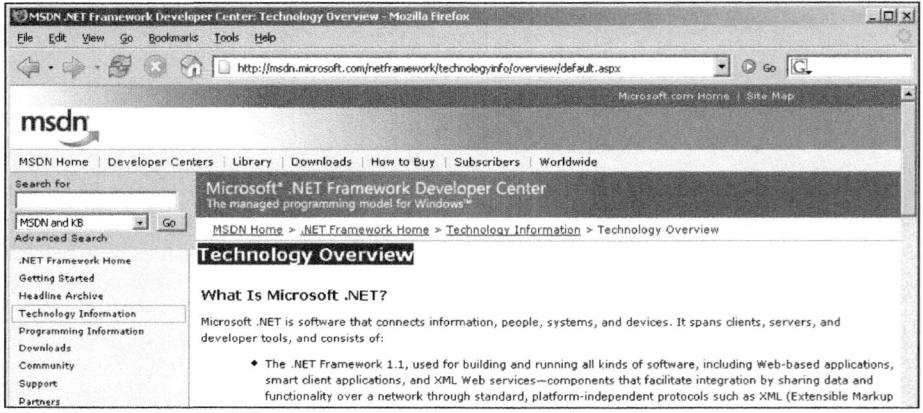

Fig. 11. Example of the framework overview provided for the .NET framework

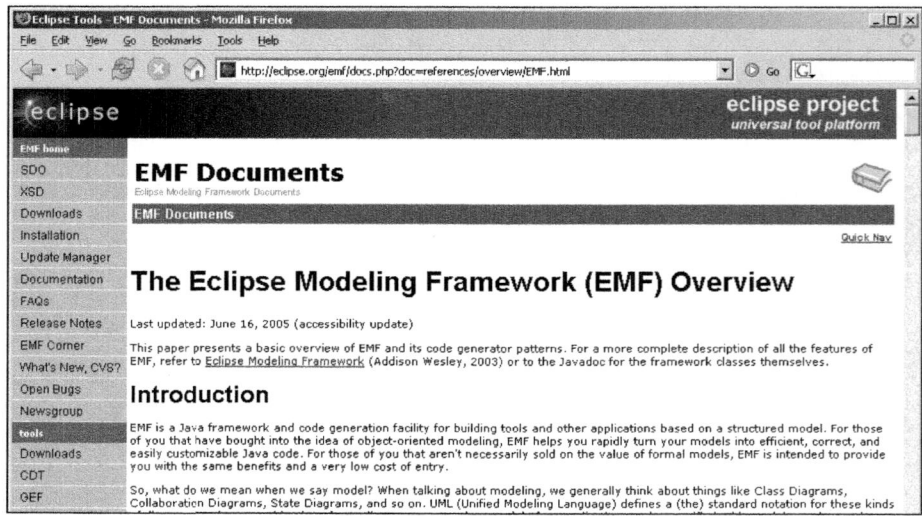

Fig. 12. Example of the overview provided with the Eclipse Modeling Framework (EMF)

.NET. The overview of the .NET framework is provided in the "Getting Started" document (Figure 8), topic "What is the .NET Framework?". A more detailed technical overview is provided in the "Technology Overview" document (Figure 10). This framework overview briefly describes the purpose of the framework, its application domain and its main components, and refers other documents containing more specific information about the framework.

EMF. The overview document of the Eclipse Modeling Framework (EMF), "Eclipse Modeling Framework Overview", is another good example (Figure 12). It is very complete and provides a brief presentation of the framework and its key features illustrated with the help of concrete examples.

5 Pattern COOKBOOK AND RECIPES

The quality of information explaining how-to-use the framework is very important to achieve its effective reuse. In most of the cases, the informal communication channels between framework developers and framework users are not available anymore, and, as a result, all information has to be communicated in alternative ways, with different kinds of manuals delivered with the framework, possibly using different media (documents, animations, videos).

Problem

To help application developers being effective on the reuse of a framework, ideally, the documentation should be organized in a way that can help readers quickly locate the explanations they strictly need to learn how to use the framework parts required to implement the specific features of the application at hands.

> **How to quickly provide users with information that helps them learning how to use the framework?**

Forces

- **Task-orientation.** Readers want to learn how to use the framework, so the documentation must focus on real tasks that users really want to perform, instead of artificial tasks, imposed by the framework.
- **Balancing Prescriptive and Descriptive information.** To be effective, the documentation must achieve a perfect balance between the level of detail of the instructions provided to guide the usage of the framework, and the level of detail and focus used to communicate how the framework works, i.e. its design internals. This perfect balance may vary with the reader of the documentation, and thus the "one size fits all" solution doesn't work here.
- **Different Audiences.** Readers of different audiences have different needs and interests that must be addressed by the documentation. New framework users want to identify, understand and manipulate the flexible features of the framework they need, as quick as possible, without being forced to understand

the detail of the whole design, but only its basic architecture (static and dynamic views). More advanced users may want to learn how to do less common customizations that possibly require a more detailed understanding of the framework's internal design.

- **Completeness.** Readers appreciate complete information, i.e., that all possible customizations are mentioned, with all the possible detail, but this is not always feasible, as it largely depends on the reader's point of view and the tasks to support.
- **Easy-to-use.** The resulting documentation must be easy to use, otherwise readers would need to spend more time than needed to browse it, and can get lost on it.
- **Cost-effectiveness.** Unfortunately, many frameworks are very complex to use and understand resulting hard, tedious and expensive to document in detail.

Solution

Provide a collection of recipes, one for each framework customization, organized in a cookbook, which acts as a guide to the contents of all its recipes.

Cookbook. A good cookbook is specific to a particular framework. Users search the cookbook for the recipe that is most appropriate for their needs, and when found, they follow the steps it describes. Recipes in a cookbook are usually organized in a spiral approach, where the most common forms of reuse are presented early, and concepts and details are delayed as long as possible. A *framework overview* is often the first recipe in a cookbook [35], being responsible for presenting the framework.

Recipe. A recipe is a document that describes how to use the framework to solve a specific problem of application development [42]. Recipes typically present information in natural language, perhaps illustrated with some pictures and code fragments. Although recipes are rather informal documents, they are usually structured in:

- a purpose section, which describes the problem the recipe is meant to solve plus some of the limitations of the solution;
- a procedure section, or how to do section, containing a sequence of the basic steps necessary to carry out the solution, and
- an examples section containing explicit, or implicit, references to models, examples and fragments of source code, and also to other related recipes.

The most important kind of information provided by cookbooks and recipes is prescriptive information that instructs users on how to use and customize the flexibility features provided by the framework. In addition, they also informally describe architectural constructs and design details, but only in a very small amount, the strictly needed to help users minimally understand what they are doing.

The best kind of documentation for beginners seems to be one that provides detailed instructions for using each individual feature of the framework without describing in detail all the theory behind them [17][39]. Considering that the main purpose of a framework is to reuse design, if it is well designed, then there must be large parts of its design that are easy to reuse even without knowing them.

On the other hand, to start using a framework without having a clear understanding of it seems to be wrong at first, but the fact is that people can't understand well a framework until they have really used it. The effective understanding of a framework thus requires that theory follows practice [39]. After the first use, the framework user has a much better understanding of what the framework does and is more capable to understand how it works, i.e. to understand its internal design details.

Related Approaches

Active cookbook. The active cookbook is a specialization of the cookbook concept that provides active guidance to framework users [39]. Active cookbooks extend the cookbook idea with a hypertext representation, a visual development environment and supporting tools. The tool support provided by active cookbooks helps the user navigate the steps of the recipes and provide the tools needed in each step, thus increasing the productivity.

Johnson's patterns. Johnson documented the HotDraw framework [39] using a pattern language comprising a set of patterns, one pattern for each recurrent problem of using the framework. The pattern language organizes the documentation, as a cookbook does with the recipes, and each pattern provides a format for each recipe.

To avoid confusion with design patterns, the term motif was later introduced in [38] to name Johnson's patterns [39]. The description of a motif has sections similar to a recipe, except that use additional references to design patterns, to provide information about the internal architecture, and references to contracts for a more rigorous description of the collaborations relevant to the motif.

Hook description. Hook descriptions were first introduced in [26] and present knowledge about framework usage, providing an alternative view to design documentation. Hook descriptions provide solutions to very well-defined problems. They detail how and where a design can be changed: what is required, the constraints to follow, and effects that the hook will impose, such as configuration constraints. A hook description usually consists of a name, the problem the hook is intended to solve, the type of adaptation used, the parts of the framework affected by the hook, other hooks required to use this hook, the participants in the hook, constraints, and comments. Hooks can be organized by hot spot: a hot spot tends to have several hooks within it. The usage of hooks can be semi-automated.

Examples

Cookbooks and recipes were historically the first technique used to document frameworks, namely the MVC framework [35] and the MacApp framework [8].

JUnit. Figure 13 presents a recipe for writing a simple test with JUnit, the first of the five recipes contained in the cookbook provided with JUnit, the "JUnit Cookbook" document [9].

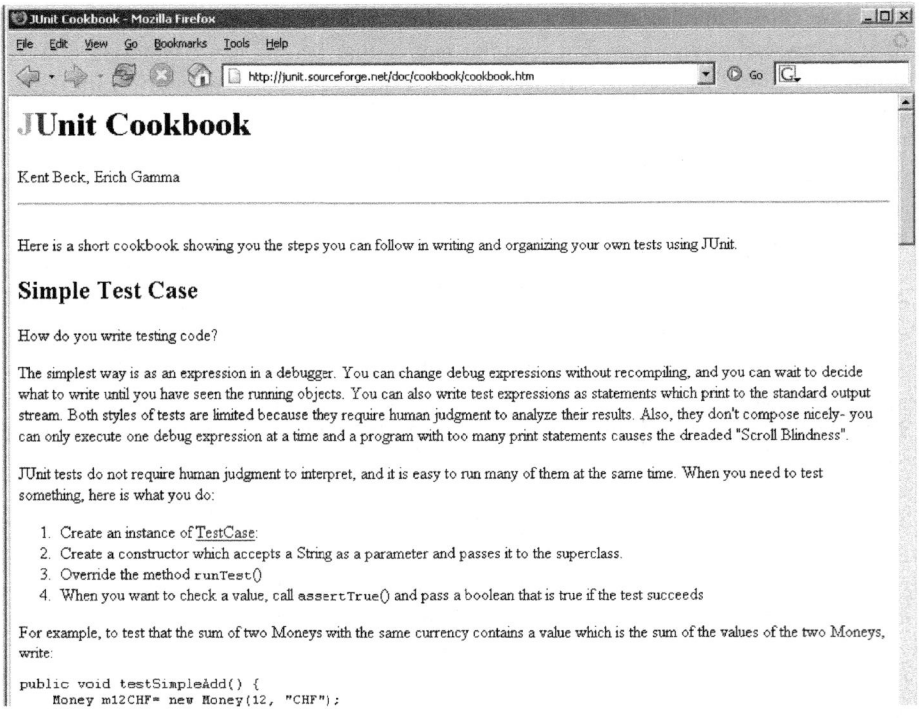

Fig. 13. Example of a recipe for writing a simple test with JUnit

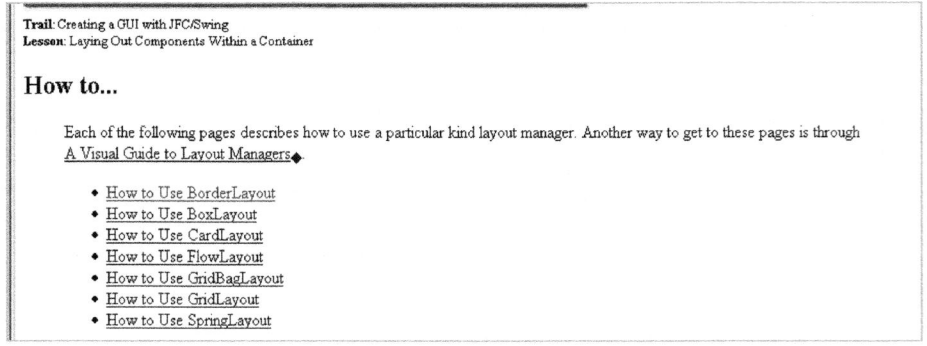

Fig. 14. Example of a cookbook from Swing framework to teach how to use layout managers

Swing. The Sun's JFC/Swing framework [20] contains several recipes organized in several cookbooks. Figure 14 shows the cookbook related with layout managers, which contains a set of recipes explaining how to use layout managers. Figure 15 shows a specific recipe explaining how to use a BorderLayout manager.

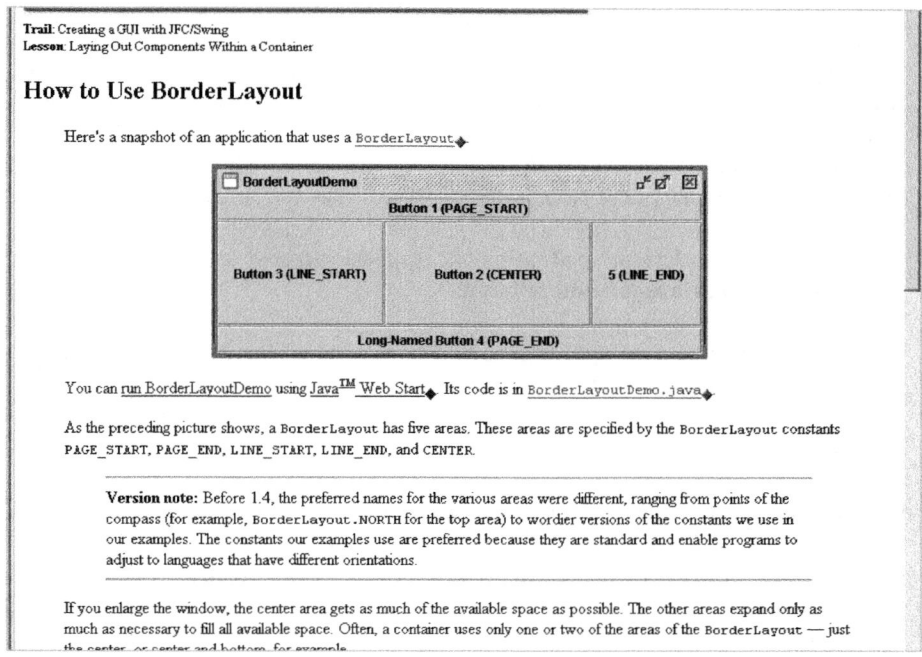

Fig. 15. Example of a recipe from Swing framework to teach how to use the BorderLayout manager

Consequences

Providing a cookbook and recipes for a framework helps on improving its task-orientation, usability, and on combining prescriptive with descriptive information.

The main audience targeted by cookbook and recipes are framework users, i.e., developers of applications intending to reuse the framework as part of it. Due to its user-orientation, this kind of documentation is usually easy to use and understand, but not complete, i.e. it doesn't intend to cover all the possible customizations with the framework but only the most relevant for the audience on target.

Because cookbook and recipes focus on teaching how-to-use a framework, it is useful to combine them with concrete or running examples, and references to the related **CUSTOMIZABLE POINTS** and source code, thus adding some redundancy, which although useful must be managed to preserve its consistency.

6   Pattern GRADED EXAMPLES

Information explaining what for a framework can be used is of great value for potential users, as it helps them to evaluate the appropriateness of the framework for the application at hands, and thus fundaments its selection, or rejection.

Problem

The first usage of a framework is always the hardest one because it may simultaneously involve the learning of the problem domain, the domain covered by the framework, and the range of solutions for which the framework was designed and is applicable. When illustrated with examples, first and subsequent usages of a framework can be easier, and more complex usages may become more interesting.

How to help readers on evaluating the appropriateness of a framework to his particular application at hands?

How to help readers on getting started fast using a framework both for simple and complex kinds of usage?

Forces

- **Task-orientation.** Framework users want practical information illustrating what can be done with the framework, and how-to-do it.
- **Different audiences.** A framework selector is someone (manager, project leader, developer) who is responsible for deciding which frameworks to use in an application development project. Among other information, framework selectors will look for the domain covered and an explanation of the most important features of the framework. New framework users want to identify, understand and manipulate the flexible features of the framework they need, as quick as possible, without being forced to understand the detail of the whole design, but only its basic architecture (static and dynamic).
- **Cost-effectiveness.** For many frameworks, the source code of example applications is the first and only documentation provided to framework users, as examples can be produced during framework development without extra effort.

Solution

Provide a small but representative graded set of training examples to illustrate the framework's applicability and features, each one illustrating a single new way of customization, smoothly growing in complexity, and eventually altogether providing complete coverage. The usage of hypertext links in the source code and the availability of executable code are valuable aids for better understanding of the examples.

Set of examples. A good set of examples, ranging from simple to complex ones, can serve as a live catalogue for the basic vocabulary of the problem domain and the key features of the framework, constituting a perfect complement to all other purposes of documentation. A proper selection of examples can be very effective for illustrating the domain covered, how-to-use the framework, and revealing some design internals. When selecting the examples to include, it is important to consider their growing level of complexity, in order to cover different levels of complexity, from low to high.

Examples. Examples play a key role in framework documentation as they make a framework more concrete; they help on understanding the flow of control, and are easier to understand than design abstractions, although less general.

The source code of example applications constructed using the framework is often the first documentation provided to application developers. Linking documents to source code and providing executable code may significantly help on understanding the examples.

The cost of producing examples to deliver with the framework is usually not high, if well planned, as the examples can also be used to drive the development, to verify the real reusability of the framework, and to help on documenting the framework.

The examples must be used to show what the framework is good for, and not for showing how to use the framework, nor for explaining how the framework is designed.

Because good examples help new users on getting started fast, the study of working examples is a nice and motivating way of learning a framework, and help drive the learning of the framework to the points of most interest to users, thus making the learning more effective.

Examples

The documentation of many successful frameworks provides a lot of examples, which make them easier to understand, to use and extend [29]. It was observed that the most typical documentation of successful frameworks includes examples that work right "out-of-the-box". Some examples are: MVC [39], ET++ [45], and Java Swing [28].

JUnit. Figure 16 presents an extract from the article "Test Infected: Programmers Love Writing Tests" [11] that uses and describes an example named `MoneyTest` provided with JUnit.

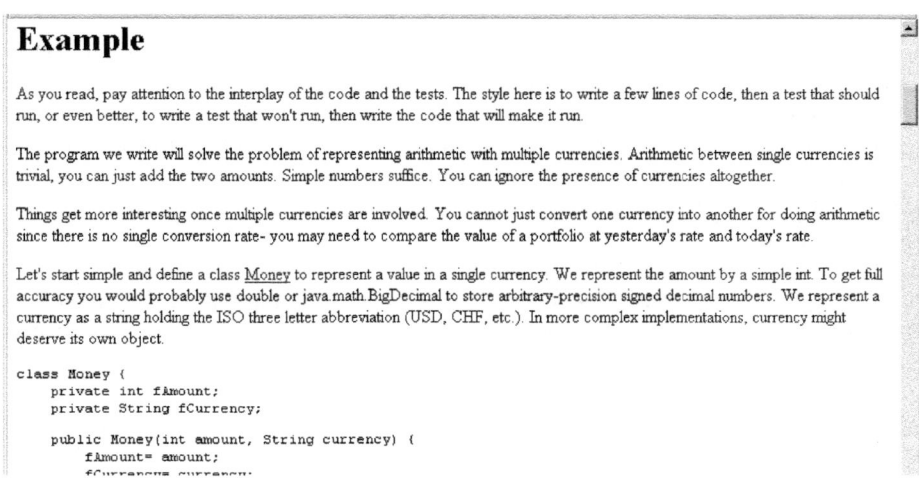

Fig. 16. MoneyTest: an example provided with JUnit

Swing. Swing provides a rich set of graded examples, very helpful for both new and experienced users on better evaluating the applicability and feasibility of the framework regarding the specific needs of the application at hands. Figure 17 shows part of a Swing tutorial fully based on examples.

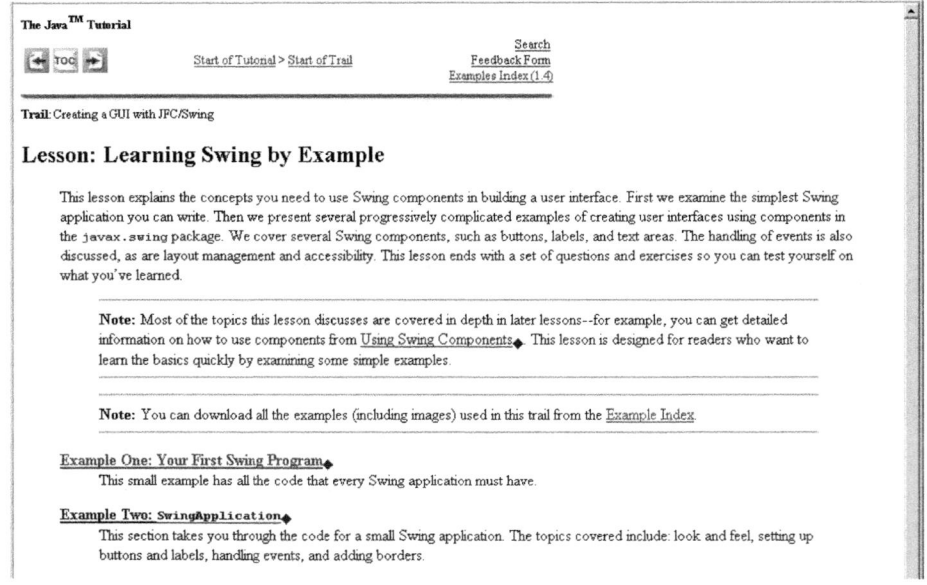

Fig. 17. An example-based tutorial provided with Swing

Consequences

Providing a good set of graded examples for a framework, ranging from simple to complex ones, is usually the less expensive kind of documentation. Examples are useful during framework development and testing, and help both new and experienced users on quickly evaluating what can be done with the framework and also reveal a little about how to use it. Examples are very task-oriented and can thus reach several audiences at the same time but they don't completely satisfy all of them (e.g. framework maintainers). Despite their value, they are however not sufficient to completely document a framework.

It is useful to include in the examples references to the **COOKBOOK & RECIPES** explaining the **CUSTOMIZABLE POINTS** used in the example, optionally referencing information about the **DESIGN INTERNALS** and source code, but this adds an extra need for maintaining the consistency of these references.

7   Pattern CUSTOMIZATION POINTS

You are documenting a framework to provide application developers with prescriptive and descriptive information capable of helping them customize the framework.

Problem

To help application developers customize a framework effectively, the documentation should be organized in a way that can help readers obtain detailed information quickly. Developers typically look for prescriptive and descriptive information to learn *which* framework parts are strictly required to customize, and *how* to customize them, to be able to implement the specific features of the application at hands.

Although examples, cookbooks and recipes are good at providing prescriptive information, they might not be sufficient to allow customization of specific parts, or in specific situations not predicted in other forms of documentation.

How to help readers know which framework parts are customizable?

How to help readers learn in detail how to customize a specific part of a framework?

Forces

- **Task-orientation.** As readers want to learn in detail how to use a certain customizable part of the framework, the documentation must focus on customization tasks imposed by the framework, which users really need to perform, as perceived in the recipes of the framework's cookbook.
- **Balancing prescriptive and descriptive information.** To be effective, the documentation describing how to customize a specific part of a framework must achieve a good balance between the level of detail of the instructions provided to guide the usage of that framework's part, and the level of detail and focus used to communicate how it works, i.e. its design internals.
- **Different audiences.** An application developer is a software engineer who is responsible for customizing a framework to produce the application at hands. Application developers want to identify which customizations are needed to produce the desired application, and to know how to implement them, instead of understanding why it must be done that way. The application developer thus needs prescriptive information capable of guiding her on finding out which hot spots must be used, which set of classes to subclass, which methods to override, and which objects to interconnect. It must be expected that the application developer possibly is not knowledgeable on the application domain and not an experienced software developer.
- **Completeness.** Readers appreciate complete information, i.e. that all possible customizations are mentioned with all the possible detail, but this is not always feasible as it largely depends on the reader's point of view and the tasks to support.
- **Easy-to-use.** Independently of the level of completeness and detail, the resulting documentation must be easy to use (clarity, easy-to understand and navigate).

Solution

Provide a list of the framework's *customization points*, also known as *hot-spots*, i.e., the points of predefined refinement where framework customization is supported, and, for each one, describe in detail the *hooks* it provides and the *hot-spot subsystem* that implements its flexibility.

To allow easy retrieval, provide lists of customization points, ideally organized by different criteria, being probably the following the most important ones:

- *by kind of framework functionality*, to provide a black-box reuse-oriented view; especially useful when looking for possibilities of customization related with a set of features in mind;

- *by framework parts and modules*, to provide a white-box reuse-oriented view; especially useful when looking for possibilities of customization related with a specific framework part or module.

Hot-spot. Customization is supported at points of predefined refinement, called *hot-spots*, using general techniques, such as: abstract classes, polymorphism and dynamic binding. A hot spot usually aggregates several hooks within it and is implemented by a hot-spot subsystem that contains base classes, concrete derived classes and possibly additional classes and relationships.

Hook. Hooks present knowledge about the usage of the framework and provide an alternative view to design documentation [26]. Hooks provide solutions to very well defined problems. They detail how and where a design can be changed: what is required, the constraints to follow, and effects that the hook will impose, such as configuration constraints.

A hook description usually consists of a name, the problem the hook is intended to solve, the type of adaptation used, the parts of the framework affected by the hook, other hooks required to use this hook, the participants in the hook, constraints, and comments. Hooks can be organized by hot spot; as said before, a hot spot tends to have several hooks within it. The usage of hooks can be semi-automated with the help of wizards, for example.

Hot-spot subsystem. The hot-spot subsystem supports variability either by inheritance or by composition. The variability is often achieved by the dynamic binding of a template method $t()$, an operation from a class T, that calls a hook method $h()$, an abstract operation from a base class, via a polymorphic reference typed with the class of the hook pointing to an operation $h'()$, from a subclass of H, that overrides $h()$. With inheritance, the polymorphic reference is attached to the hot-spot subsystem; with composition the reference is contained in it. Figure 18 below shows an example of both kinds of hot-spot subsystems.

Examples

Despite providing an organized list of customization points being of great value in terms of documentation completeness, they are not so frequently used as examples, cookbooks and recipes in the documentation of the most popular frameworks, namely those we have been referring so far in these patterns. We discuss below how these customizations are documented in some well-known frameworks.

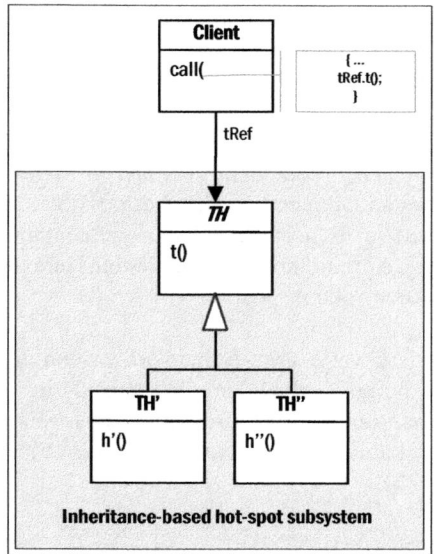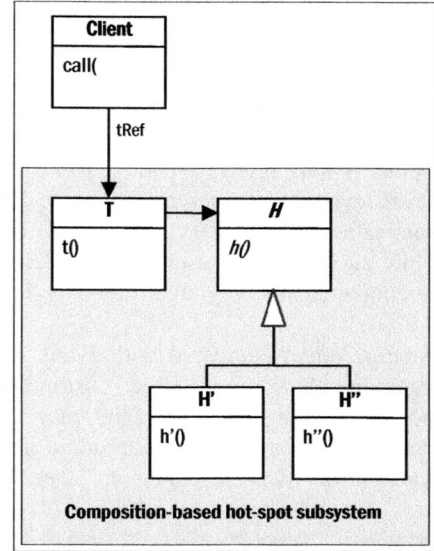

Fig. 18. Inheritance-based and composition-based hot-spot subsystems

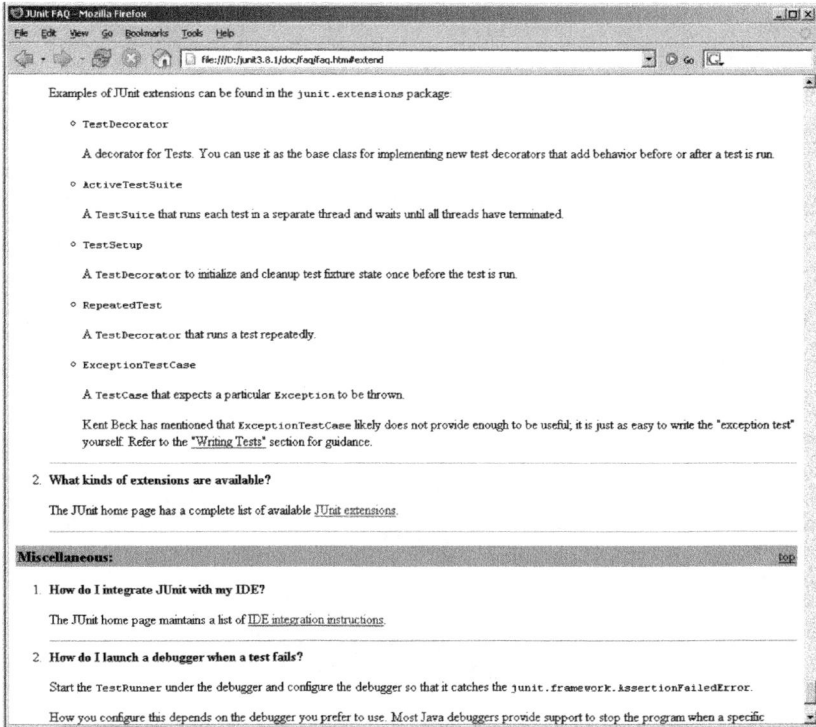

Fig. 19. JUnit: hot-spots are only implicitly mentioned in the FAQ

JUnit. The major kind of reuse that JUnit was designed for is very simple and consists only on writing and organizing tests, so its documentation is mostly targeted to explain how to do these tasks, which is simply and perfectly documented as cookbooks and recipes in the document "JUnit Cookbook" document [9].

However, some more customizations can be done with JUnit, such as test runners, and test decorators, but information about these and other less used customization points is only briefly mentioned in the "JUnit FAQ" document [18] and in the low-level Javadoc documentation. Figure 19 shows an enumeration of other possible customizations of JUnit (version 3.8.2) described in its accompanying documentation. How such customizations are implemented, i.e. their hot-spot subsystems are not documented and only identifiable by direct source code inspection.

Swing. When compared with JUnit, Swing is a very large framework providing a huge number of possible customization points, which are organized in its documentation in a simple and easy to browse manner that uses different levels of depth and detail. The most intuitive list is probably the one provided by the "Visual Index to the Swing Components" (see Figure 20).

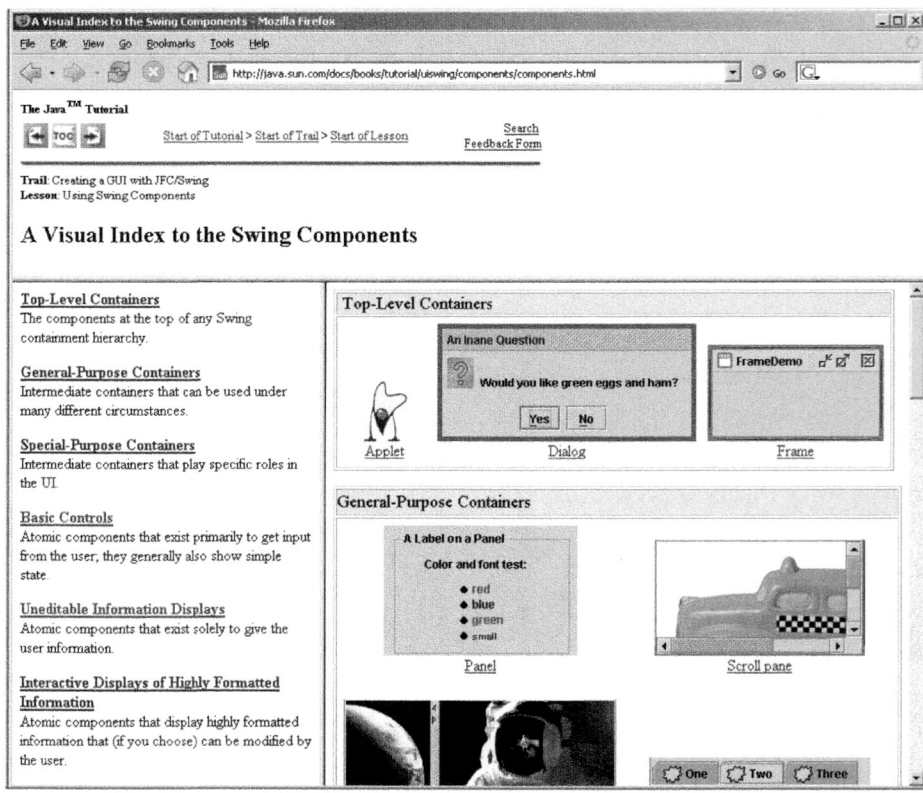

Fig. 20. "A Visual Index to the Swing Components"

A good and more complete alternative to the visual index to learn what can be cus-
tomized in the Swing framework is the list that enumerates how-to use each of the key
components (Figure 21-left), which gives access to more detailed lists of possible
customizations of each component (Figure 21-right). Even more detailed information
about how the flexibility is supported in each customization point although not explicit in the documentation, is left to the reader to explore by herself, probably using
the Javadoc comments and source code inspection.

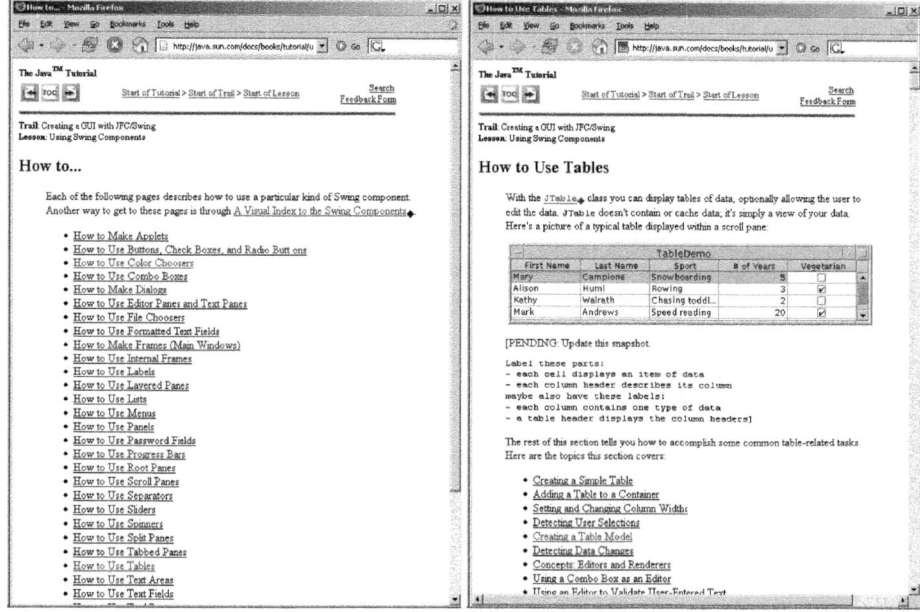

Fig. 21. List of the most frequently used customizations possible with Swing and Tables

Consequences

By providing framework users with an organized and exhaustive list of all the predefined customization points, or at least, the most important and frequently used, readers
can evaluate if the framework is applicable to the problems at hands, and therefore to
decide with more confidence whether or not to reuse it.

After knowing the points to customize, whether the knowledge was gathered from
own experience, others' knowledge, or documentation (e.g. **CUSTOMIZATION
POINTS**, **GRADED EXAMPLES**, or **COOKBOOKS & RECIPES**), framework users can
then start learning which tasks must be carried on to customize them properly, possibly supported by the prescriptive information provided by the **COOKBOOKS & RECI-
PES** related with those customization points. In addition, they can use the descriptive
information provided for each **CUSTOMIZATION POINT** to learn more about how its
flexibility is supported, and the information about its **DESIGN INTERNALS** to know in
detail how the framework is designed.

Although adding some possible redundancy, lists of CUSTOMIZATION POINTS are easy to use and browse and provide a good balance between prescriptive and descriptive information thus being a good complement to the prescriptive information of COOKBOOKS & RECIPES and the descriptive information of DESIGN INTERNALS.

8   Pattern DESIGN INTERNALS

Information explaining in detail how a framework was designed and implemented can be of great value for potential users willing to get a better understanding on how to reuse it in advanced ways.

Problem

Framework instantiation for a particular application often requires customizing hot spots in a way planned by framework designers. Typical instantiations can be often achieved simply by plugging in concrete classes selected from an existing library that customize the hot spots to the needs of the application at hands, also known as black-box reuse. Other instantiations can be achieved by extending framework abstract classes in a way planned by framework designers. The instantiation requires matching of interfaces and behaviors, and the writing of code to implement new behaviors, also known as white-box reuse.

Not all instantiations of a framework are simple to achieve, but they can't be all documented exhaustively and in enough detail, especially those more advanced customizations, or those not initially planned by framework developers.

To cover these advanced instantiations, and also other kinds of reuse, such as flexing, composing, evolving or mining a framework, it is thus important to provide framework users with detailed information about how a framework and its flexibility was designed and implemented.

> **How to help framework users on quickly grasping the design and implementation of a framework to support them on achieving advanced customizations, not typical, or not specifically documented?**

Forces

- **Different purposes.** In addition to the framework purpose and usage instructions, the documentation must also help framework users on understanding the underlying principles and the basic architecture of the framework. With such detailed information, users are able to develop not only trivial and planned applications, but also advanced ones, that are conformant to the framework.
- **Balancing prescriptive and descriptive information.** Although programmers can use a framework without completely understanding how it works, such as when following a set of instructions, a framework is much more useful for those who understand it in detail. To be effective, the documentation must achieve a perfect balance between the level of detail of the instructions provided, to guide the usage of the framework, and the level of detail used to communicate how the framework works, i.e. its design internals.

- **Minimizing design information complexity.** To communicate complex software designs is challenging. Frameworks derive their flexibility and reusability from the use (and abuse) of interfaces and abstract classes, which, together with polymorphic methods, significantly complicate the understanding of the run-time architecture. The design information to communicate may include not only the different classes of the framework, but also the strategic roles and collaborations of their instances, rules and constraints, such as cardinality of framework objects, creation and destruction of static and dynamic framework objects, instantiation order, and synchronization and performance issues.

Solution

Provide concise detailed information about the design internals of the framework, especially the areas designed to support configuration, known as hot-spots. You should start by describing how the framework hot-spots support configuration. This can be done, for example, by describing the roles of framework participants using *design patterns* and *design pattern instantiations*, or at a meta-level using *meta-patterns*, or, even at source-code level.

Design pattern instances. Searching, selecting and applying design patterns are the necessary steps of the cognitive process for assigning the roles defined in a pattern to concrete classes, responsibilities, methods and attributes of the concrete design. This process is generally called pattern instantiation [40].

Documenting pattern instances is important because it will help other developers on better understanding the resulting concrete classes, attributes and methods, and the underneath design decisions. This provides a level of abstraction higher than the class level, highlighting the commonalities of the system and thus promoting the understandability, conciseness and consistency of the documentation. At the same time, the documentation of pattern instances will help the designer instantiating a pattern, to certify that she is taking the right decision. In general, this results in better communication within the development team and consequently on less bugs.

To more formally document a pattern instance we must describe the design context, justify the selection of the pattern, explain how the pattern's roles, operations and associations are mapped to the concrete design classes, and to state the benefits and liabilities of instantiating the pattern, eventually in comparison with other alternatives.

Design patterns. A pattern names, abstracts, and identifies the key aspects of a design structure commonly used to solve a recurrent problem. Succinctly, a *pattern* is a generic *solution* to a recurring *problem* in a given *context* [6]. The description of a pattern explains the problem and its context, suggests a generic solution, and discusses the consequences of adopting that solution.

The solution describes the objects and classes that participate in the design, their responsibilities and collaborations. The concepts of pattern and pattern language were introduced in the software community by the influence of the Christopher Alexander's work, an architect who wrote extensively on patterns found in the architecture of houses, buildings and communities [6]. Patterns help to abstract the design process and to reduce the complexity of software because patterns specify abstractions at a higher level than single classes and objects. This higher-level is usually referred as the *pattern level*.

A design pattern is thus a specialization of the pattern concept for the domain of software design. Design patterns capture expert solutions to recurring design problems. As design patterns provide an abstraction above the level of classes and objects, they are suggested as a natural way for documenting frameworks [39]: to describe the purpose of the framework, the rationale behind design decisions, and to teach them to their potential users.

Design patterns are particularly good for documenting frameworks because they capture design experience at the micro-architecture level and capture meta-knowledge about how to incorporate flexibility [27][13]. In fact, design patterns are capable of illuminating and motivating architectures, preserve design decisions made by original designers and communicate to future users, and provide a common vocabulary that improves design communication, and to help on the understanding of the dynamics of control flow.

The concepts of frameworks and patterns are closely related, but neither subordinate to the other. Frameworks are usually composed of many design patterns, but are much more complex than a single design pattern. In relation to design patterns, a framework is sometimes defined as an implementation of a collection of design patterns.

To document the design internals of a framework in relation with the patterns it implements we must first know, or recognize, the patterns in the framework design, and to match them against the many popular design patterns already documented, such as the catalogues known as GoF patterns [27] and POSA patterns [14]. However, more contextualized design patterns are very likely to not being yet published or documented, due to its specificity, either in terms of applicability or organization dependency. In these situations, it is required to spend the effort to mine and write the patterns considered important to explain the underlying framework design. A good source of knowledge for those willing to learn how to write patterns is [39], itself documented under the form of a pattern language.

Meta-patterns. Frameworks are designed to provide their flexibility at hot spots using two essential constructs: templates and hooks. The possible ways of composing template and hook classes in the hot spots of a framework were catalogued and presented under the form of a set of design patterns, which were called meta-patterns. Although meta-patterns can be used to document the roles of framework participants, the level of detail is too fine to be useful, but extremely useful to document the roles of the participants involved in a design pattern [42].

Examples

Design patterns are commonly used to document the global architecture of the framework. We will illustrate here with examples of how design patterns are used to document popular frameworks, such as JUnit, Swing, J2EE and .NET, and also the classical HotDraw framework.

HotDraw. The first paper that mentions the advantages of using patterns to document a framework is authored by Ralph Johnson [39], which presents a pattern language to document the HotDraw framework, comprising a set of patterns, one for each recurrent problem of using the framework. In that work, patterns are not only used to document the design of the framework, but also as a way of organizing the documentation, similarly as a cookbook does with the recipes (pattern **COOKBOOK & RECIPES**), where each pattern provides a format for each recipe.

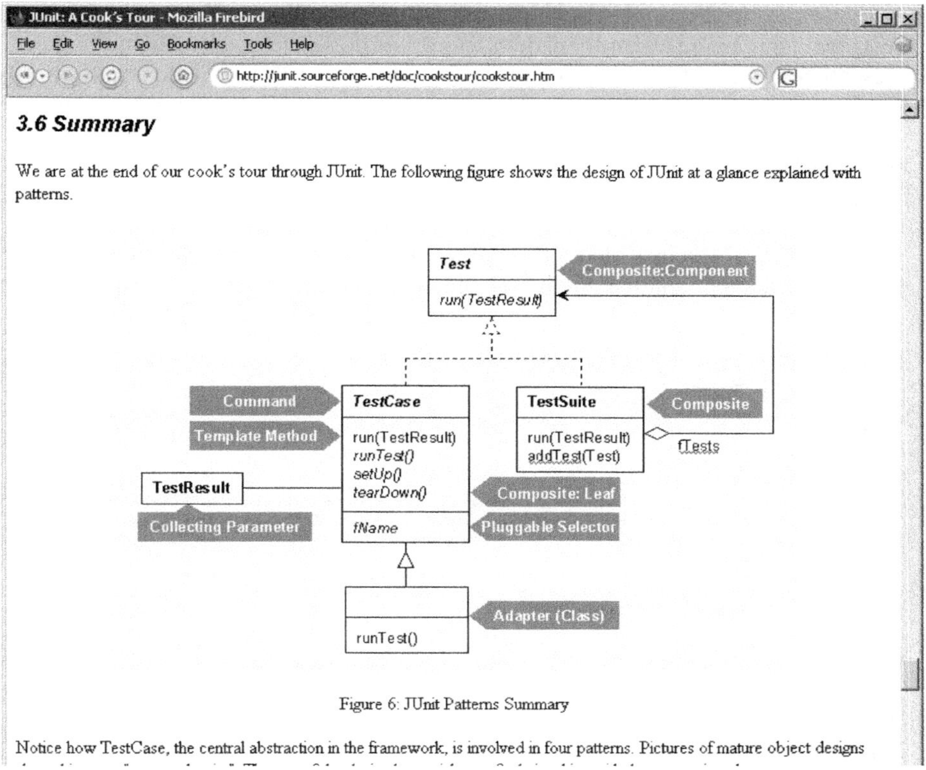

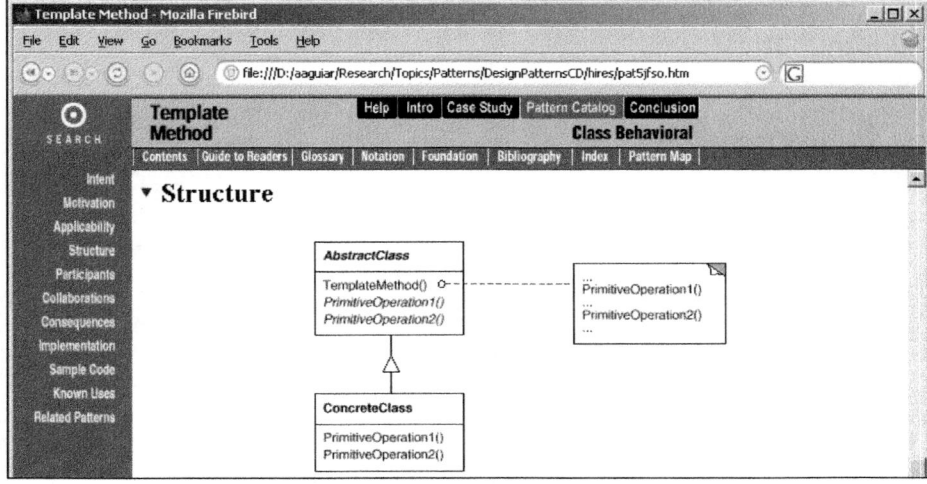

Fig. 22. Example of using design patterns to document the design of JUnit

Fig. 23. Template Method Pattern

JUnit. The document "A Cook's Tour" [12], devoted to explain how JUnit was designed, includes a pattern-by-pattern tour to the design internals of JUnit. Figure 22 presents an extract from this document that shows the design patterns used in the architecture of JUnit, which describe in more detail JUnit's internal design. In concrete, it informally enumerates the design patterns instantiated by the major abstractions of JUnit.

Figure 23 presents another extract from this document informally explaining, using natural language, models, and fragments of source code, how the class `TestCase` instantiates the Template Method design pattern. Figure 23 presents an extract from the documentation relative to the Template Method pattern [27] that shows the

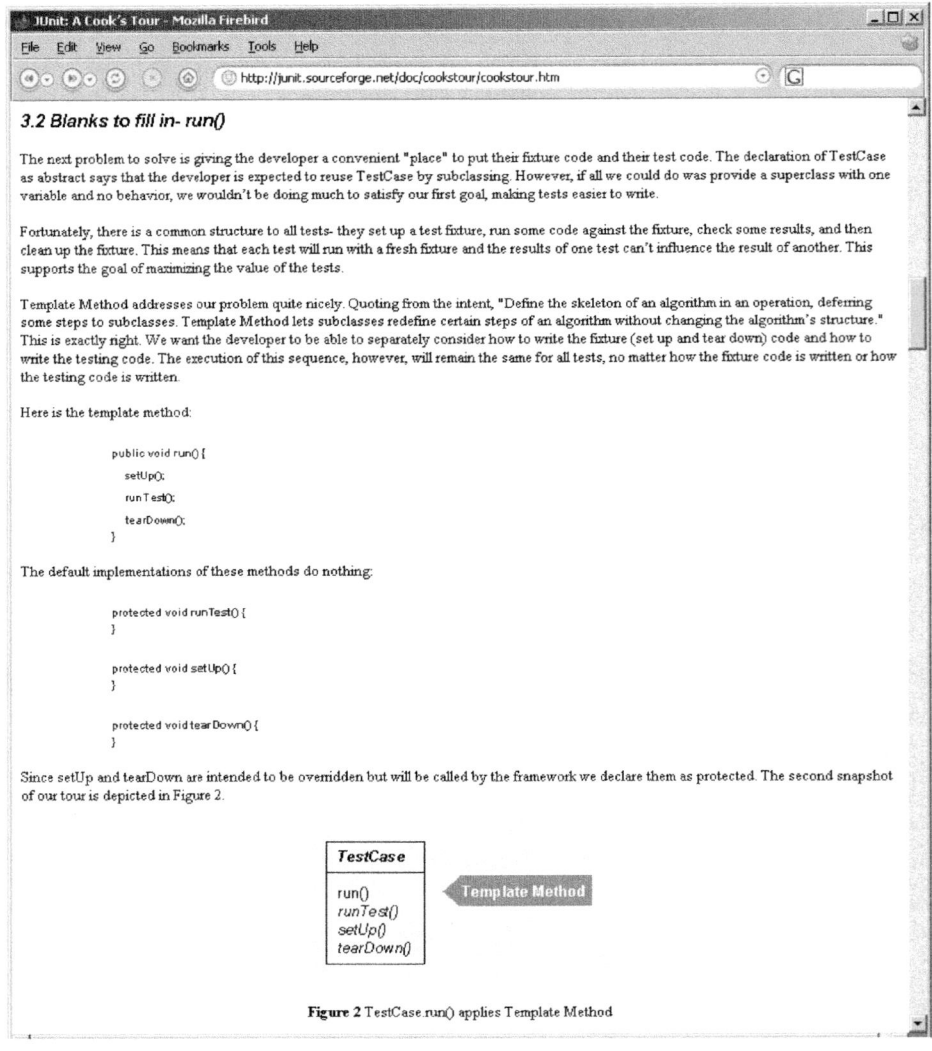

Fig. 24. Template Method being instantiated by the TestCase class

structure of the solution proposed by the pattern, the participants involved and their roles, and the consequences of instantiating the pattern.

Known Uses

Swing. The much more complex Swing framework instantiates many more patterns (e.g. Observer, Composite, Decorator, Visitor, etc.) but its accompanying documentation doesn't use pattern instances as explicitly and exhaustively as we can observe in JUnit, probably due to the cost of doing it.

Figure 25 shows an extract from an overview of the Swing architecture, where we can learn about the foundational design principles of Swing, concretely the model-view-controller architectural pattern (MVC) and its instantiation in Swing classes.

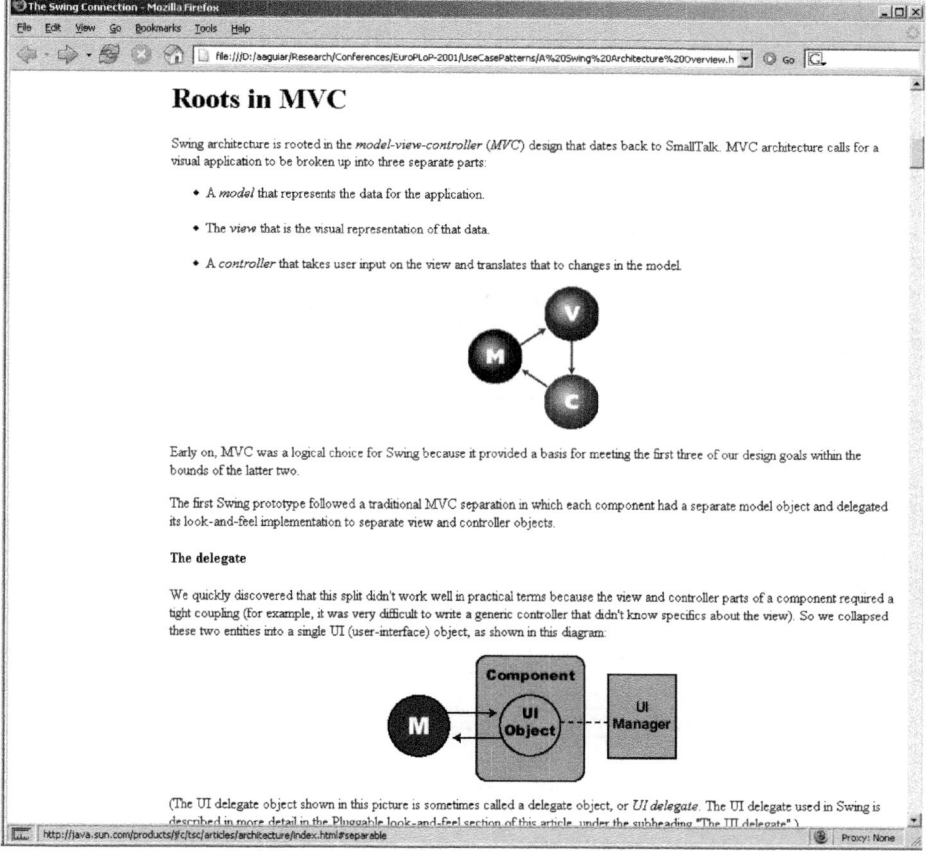

Fig. 25. An extract from "A Swing architecture overview" showing MVC and its instantiation in Swing

J2EE. The patterns underlying the design of the enterprise version of Java is documented in the core J2EE patterns catalog [7], which serve as a valuable source of knowledge to learn more about how J2EE is designed and how the applications based on J2EE should be designed. Figure 26 shows the index of all the core J2EE patterns.

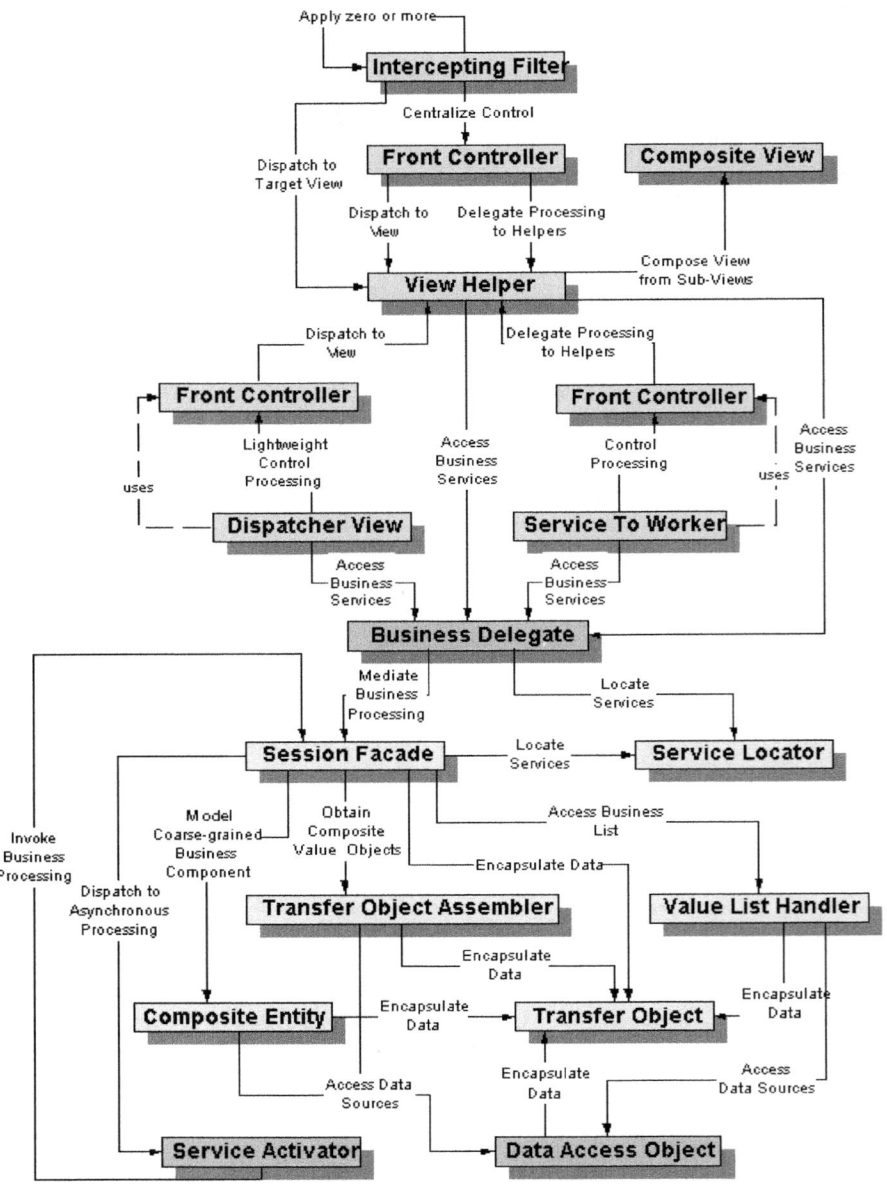

Fig. 26. Core J2EE Patterns: patterns index

.NET. Similarly to J2EE, there is a document that presents the patterns underlying Microsoft's .NET framework for enterprise applications. Figure 27 shows the documentation of the MVC pattern, which includes an example of its instantiation in .NET.

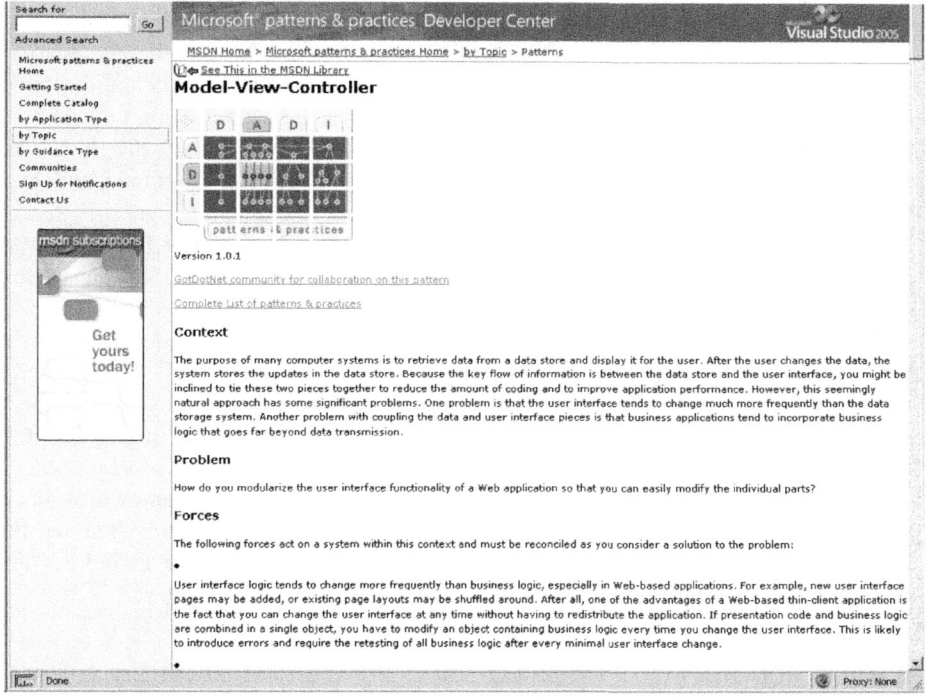

Fig. 27. .NET enterprise solution patterns" showing MVC and its instantiation in .NET

Consequences

By documenting the framework design internals, using patterns and pattern instances, namely, we provide framework users with additional knowledge that can help them better understand the underlying architecture and design principles of the framework, and therefore to enable more advanced customizations or simple but not documented customizations elsewhere in another form of documentation.

However, to document framework's specific patterns, not published, and to document pattern instances can be hard work, if not done at the right moment by the right people.

As one of the most complex kinds of object-oriented software systems, frameworks can be hard to understand and explain, but definitely patterns are a excellent mean to do that, as they provide a good balancing between simplicity of reading and richness of the information provided.

9 Conclusions

Good documentation is crucial for effective framework reuse, but, unfortunately, it is often hard, costly, and tiresome, coming with many issues.

In this paper, we present a set of patterns that capture proven solutions to recurrent problems of documenting object-oriented frameworks. These patterns are part of the results of a large study based on existing literature, case studies and lessons learned, lead by the authors, aiming at helping to improve framework documentation. Other results include a documentation approach and wiki-based documentation tools [1].

The patterns here presented were selected as the most important for the framework documentation itself, here seen as an autonomous and tangible product independent of the process used to create it. Along with these patterns, the essential concepts, forces, and tradeoffs are also described, including information about the different types of documents, audiences, roles, activities, key issues and best practices, thus constituting a solid starting base for those willing to learn about how to document a framework.

The present version of these patterns are a result of several refinements in order to simplify , prescribe simple solutions that can be applied as needed, inexpensively, being easy to follow, incremental, and containing the essential to document object-oriented frameworks effectively. Additional patterns might be used to address other issues of documenting frameworks.

For those already familiar with the problematic of documenting frameworks, or reusable software, these patterns provide a survey on the topic and a consolidation. For those new to the topic, these patterns provide simple but important guidelines that enable them to document a framework in a systematic and effective way.

Acknowledgements

The authors would like to thank all those involved in the shepherding of the patterns in this document, both for having pushed forward the writing of this pattern language and for the valuable comments and feedback provided: Neil Harrison, for Viking-PLoP'2005; Uwe Zdun, for EuroPLoP'2006; Rosana Teresinha Vaccare Braga and Ralph Johnson, for PLoP'2006.

We would like to thank also the participants of the writers' workshops at Viking-PLoP'2005, EuroPLoP'2006, and PLoP'2006, for their comments and suggestions for improvement: Juha Parssinen, Sami Lehtonen, Eduardo Fernandez, Kevlin Henney, Klaus Marquardt, Sergiy Alpaev, Uwe Zdun, Allan Kelly, Ian Graham, Alexander Fülleborrnand, Martin Schmettow, Michalis Hadjisimouand, Ward Cunningham, Sachin Bammi, Philipp Bachmann, Andrew Black, Brian Foote, Maurice Rabb, Daniel Vainsencher, Anders, Mirko Raner, and Kanwardeep Ahluwalia. In addition, we are grateful to Richard Gabriel, Joseph Yoder, Mark Perry, and Maria for the feedback provided to other patterns not included in this document, but closely related, addressing process issues. Finally, we thank all those contributed with their precious reviews of this work.

References

[1] Aguiar, A.: A minimalist approach to framework documentation. PhD thesis, Faculdade de Engenharia da Universidade do Porto (2003)

[2] Aguiar, A., David, G.: Patterns for Documenting Frameworks – Part I. In: Proceedings of VikingPLoP 2005, Helsinki, Finland (2005) (to be published)

[3] Aguiar, A., David, G.: Patterns for Documenting Frameworks – Part II. In: Proceedings of EuroPLoP 2006, Irsee, Germany (2006)

[4] Aguiar, A., David, G.: Patterns for Documenting Frameworks – Part III. In: Proceedings of PLoP 2006, Portland, Oregon, USA (2006)

[5] Aguiar, A., David, G.: Patterns for Documenting Frameworks – Process. In: Proceedings of SugarLoafPLoP 2007, Porto de Galinhas, Recife, Pernambuco, Brazil (2007)

[6] Alexander, C., Ishikawa, S., Silverstein, M.: A Pattern Language. Oxford University Press, Oxford (1977)

[7] Alur, D., Crupi, J., Malks, D.: Core J2EE Patterns: Best Practices and Design Strategies, 1st edn. Prentice Hall / Sun Microsystems Press (2001) ISBN:0130648841

[8] Apple Computer, MacApp Programmer's Guide. Apple Computer (1986)

[9] Beck, K., Gamma, E.: JUnit homepage (1997), http://www.junit.org

[10] Beck, K., Gamma, E.: JUnit: Cookbook (2003b), http://junit.sourceforge.net/doc/cookbook/cookbook.htm

[11] Beck, K., Gamma, E.: JUnit: Test infected: Programmers love writing tests (2003c), http://junit.sourceforge.net/doc/testinfected/testing.htm

[12] Beck, K., Gamma, E.: JUnit: A cook's tour (2003a), http://junit.sourceforge.net/doc/cookstour/cookstour.htm

[13] Beck, K., Johnson, R.: Patterns generate architectures, vol. 821, pp. 139–149. Springer, Berlin (1994)

[14] Buschmann, F., Meunier, R., Rohnert, H., Sommerlad, P., Stal, M.: Pattern Oriented Software Architecture — a System of Patterns. John Wiley & Sons, Chichester (1996)

[15] Butler, G.: A reuse case perspective on documenting frameworks (1997), http://www.cs.concordia.ca/faculty/gregb

[16] Butler, G., Keller, R.K., Mili, H.: A framework for framework documentation. ACM Comput. Surv. 32(1es):15 (2000)

[17] Carroll, J.M.: The Nurnberg Funnel: Designing Minimalist Instruction for Practical Computer Skill. MIT Press, Cambridge (1990)

[18] Clark, M.: JUnit: FAQ - frequently asked questions (2003), http://junit.sourceforge.net/doc/faq/faq.htm

[19] Cotter, S., Potel, M.: Inside Taligent Technology. Addison-Wesley, Reading (1995)

[20] Demeyer, S., De Hondt, K., Steyaert, P.: Consistent framework documentation with computed links and framework contracts. ACM Comput. Surv., 32(1es), 34 (2000)

[21] Eckstein, R., Loy, M., Wood, D.: Java Swing. O'Reilly & Associates, Inc., Sebastopol (1998)

[22] FEUP, doc-it project web site, http://doc-it.fe.up.pt/

[23] Fayad, M.E., Johnson, R.E.: Domain-Specific Application Frameworks — Frameworks Experience by Industry. John Wiley & Sons, Chichester (2000)

[24] Fayad, M.E., Schmidt, D.C., Johnson, R.E.: Building Application Frameworks — Object-Oriented Foundations of Framework Design. John Wiley & Sons, Chichester (1999a)

[25] Fayad, M.E., Schmidt, D.C., Johnson, R.E.: Implementing Application Frameworks — Object-Oriented Frameworks at Work. John Wiley & Sons, Chichester (1999b)

[26] Froehlich, G., Hoover, H.J., Liu, L., Sorenson, P.G.: Hooking into object-oriented application frameworks. In: International Conference on Software Engineering, pp. 491–501 (1997)

[27] Gamma, E., Helm, R., Johnson, R., Vlissides, J.: Design Patterns — Elements of reusable object-oriented software. Addison-Wesley, Reading (1995b)

[28] Gosling, J., Joy, B., Steele Jr., G.L.: The Java Language Specification. Addison-Wesley, Reading (1996), http://java.sun.com/docs/books/jls/

[29] Hansen, T.: Development of successful object-oriented frameworks. In: Addendum to the 1997 ACM SIGPLAN Conference on Object-Oriented Programming, Systems, Languages, and Applications (Addendum), pp. 115–119. ACM Press, New York (1997)

[30] Hargis, G.: Developing quality technical information, 2nd edn. Prentice-Hall, Englewood Cliffs (2004)

[31] IBM Corporation. Producing quality technical information. IBM Santa Teresa Laboratory (1983)

[32] Johnson, R.: Documenting frameworks using patterns. In: Paepcke, A. (ed.) OOPSLA 1992 Conference Proceedings, pp. 63–76. ACM Press, New York (1992)

[33] Johnson, R.E., Foote, B.: Designing reusable classes. Journal of Object-Oriented Programming 1(2), 22–35 (1988)

[34] Johnson, R.E., Russo, V.F.: Reusing object-oriented design. Technical Report Technical Report UIUCDCS 91-1696, University of Illinois (1991)

[35] Kirk, D.: Framework reuse: Process, problems and documentation. Technical Report EFoCS-43-2001, Department of Computer Science, University of Strathclyde, GLASGOW, UK (2001), http://www.cis.strath.ac.uk/research/efocs/

[36] Kirk, D., Roper, M., Wood, M.: Understanding object oriented frameworks: An exploratory case study. Technical Report EFoCS-42-2001, Department of Computer Science, University of Strathclyde, GLASGOW, UK (2001), http://www.cis.strath.ac.uk/research/efocs/

[37] Krasner, G.E., Pope, S.T.: A cookbook for using the model-view-controller user interface paradigm in smalltalk-80. Journal of Object-Oriented Programming 1(3), 27–49 (1988)

[38] Lajoie, R., Keller, R.K.: Design and reuse in object-oriented frameworks: Patterns, contracts and motifs in concert, pp. 295–312. World Scientific Publishing, Singapore (1995)

[39] Meszaros, G., Doble, J.: Metapatterns: A pattern language for pattern writing. In: The 3rd Pattern Languages of Programming Conference, Monticello, Illinois (September 1996)

[40] Meusel, M., Czarnecki, K., Köpf, W.: A model for structuring user documentation of object-oriented frameworks using patterns and hypertext. In: Liu, Y., Auletta, V. (eds.) ECOOP 1997. LNCS, vol. 1241, pp. 496–510. Springer, Heidelberg (1997)

[41] Odenthal, G., Quibeldey-Cirkel, K.: Using patterns for design and documentation. In: Akcsit, M., Matsuoka, S. (eds.) ECOOP 1997. LNCS, vol. 1241, pp. 511–529. Springer, Heidelberg (1997)

[42] Pree, W.: Design Patterns for Object-Oriented Software Development. Addison-Wesley / ACM Press (1995)

[43] Schappert, A., Sommerlad, P., Pree, W.: Automated support for software development with frameworks. In: ACM SIGSOFT Symposium on Software Reusability, pp. 123–127 (1995)

[44] Press, T.: The Power of Frameworks: for Windows and OS/2 developers. Addison-Wesley, Reading (1995)

[45] Weinand, A., Gamma, E., Marty, R.: Design and implementation of ET++, a seamless object-oriented application framework. Structured Programming 10(2) (1989)

Author Index

GPSR Compliance

The European Union's (EU) General Product Safety Regulation (GPSR) is a set of rules that requires consumer products to be safe and our obligations to ensure this.

If you have any concerns about our products, you can contact us on ProductSafety@springernature.com

In case Publisher is established outside the EU, the EU authorized representative is:

Springer Nature Customer Service Center GmbH
Europaplatz 3
69115 Heidelberg, Germany

Batch number: 09490872

Printed by Printforce, the Netherlands

Lecture Notes in Computer Science 6510

Commenced Publication in 1973
Founding and Former Series Editors:
Gerhard Goos, Juris Hartmanis, and Jan van Leeuwen

Editorial Board